Wondrous Reading

Wondrous Reading

Encountering the Catholic Faith in Children's Literature

LuElla D'Amico

CASCADE *Books* • Eugene, Oregon

WONDROUS READING
Encountering the Catholic Faith in Children's Literature

Copyright © 2025 LuElla D'Amico. All rights reserved. Except for brief quotations in critical publications or reviews, no part of this book may be reproduced in any manner without prior written permission from the publisher. Write: Permissions, Wipf and Stock Publishers, 199 W. 8th Ave., Suite 3, Eugene, OR 97401.

Cascade Books
An Imprint of Wipf and Stock Publishers
199 W. 8th Ave., Suite 3
Eugene, OR 97401

www.wipfandstock.com

PAPERBACK ISBN: 979-8-3852-1483-9
HARDCOVER ISBN: 979-8-3852-1484-6
EBOOK ISBN: 979-8-3852-1485-3

Cataloguing-in-Publication data:

Names: D'Amico, LuElla, author.

Title: Wondrous reading : Encountering the Catholic faith in children's literature / LuElla D'Amico.

Description: Eugene, OR: Cascade Books, 2025 | Includes bibliographical references and index.

Identifiers: ISBN 979-8-3852-1483-9 (paperback) | ISBN 979-8-3852-1484-6 (hardcover) | ISBN 979-8-3852-1485-3 (ebook)

Subjects: LCSH: Children—Books and reading. | Oral reading. | Faith formation—Christianity—Roman Catholicism.

Classification: LB1573 D36 2025 (paperback) | LB1573 (ebook)

VERSION NUMBER 11/20/25

Dedicated to Jack and Emmeline,
who remind me to gaze with wonder every day.

"Within every one of these children's heads there is a new universe, as new as it was on the seventh day of creation. In each of those orbs, there is a new system of stars, new grass, new cities, a new sea."

G. K. Chesterton

"We will not hide them from their descendants; we will tell the next generation the praiseworthy deeds of the Lord, his power, and the wonders he has done."

(Psalm 78:4)

Contents

Acknowledgments | ix

How to Read This Book | 1

Introduction: Reading for the Soul: Growing in
    Faith Through Children's Literature | 7

1 Liturgical Living in *The Giving Tree* and *Cecilia's Magical Mission* | 26
2 The Interplay of Faith and Reason in *Goodnight Moon* and the Magic Tree House Series | 43
3 Culture of Life in *Alma and How She Got Her Name* and *Little Women* | 66
4 Care of God's Creation in *The Snowy Day* and *The Wind in the Willows* | 91

Epilogue: Reading Wondrously | 109

Appendix | 113
Bibliography | 141
Index | 145

Acknowledgments

WHEN THE COVID-19 PANDEMIC hit, I realized my career was not where I wanted it to be. As a professor, that does not mean I wasn't publishing in the academic journals I wanted to or that I wasn't teaching students whom I cared about deeply. Rather, I felt adrift because the Holy Spirit didn't seem to be guiding my career, and I wasn't sure where I should be going.

It was my husband, Scott, who mentioned to me in our living room one day while I was bemoaning my future that I should write a book combining my passion and expertise in children's literature with my love for the Catholic faith. I stared at him, thought about it, and said, "I don't think that's the right direction." I had never written anything expressly about my faith in a public way, and I automatically thought that it would be awkward, given how much of a private person I was at the time. (Those who know me now can feel free to laugh here.)

A week later, Tim O'Malley, a friend I'd made, came to visit to speak at the university in Texas where I teach. He was the first person I'd seen besides my family since the pandemic started. While sitting in my office, awkwardly (I hadn't seen anyone besides my family in a very long time because of the pandemic), I took this opportunity to bemoan my career anyway, raising the awkwardness of the situation to new levels without hesitation (as I am sometimes apt to do). Like my husband, he said, "Why don't you write a book about Catholicism and children's literature?" Cue the previous week's theme song. I stared at him, thought about it, and said, "I don't think that's the right direction."

The Holy Spirit moves one's heart, though, and I kept thinking about what both my husband and Tim said off and on for the next few months. I kept reading aloud with my children, too. That spring, I was scheduled to

Acknowledgments

teach one of my regular courses at my university, Children's Literature. It was one of my favorite iterations of the classes I've ever taught. The students were not only engaged but were asking deep questions about the Catholic faith in the stories we read, wanting to know more. I juggled numerous independent projects about this very topic. Soon, I knew I was called to write this book, and I began working on a proposal for it. I also began writing about my faith in more public venues, knowing I wanted my writing to reach audiences outside of the academy.

First, most importantly, then, I want to thank my husband, Scott, who always seems to see the right path I should take before I do. Marrying well has always been the greatest blessing of my life. Scott has read much of this book, and he has read far more children's books than he ever imagined he would in his life. Moreover, he has watched our children while much of this book has been written. *Wondrous Reading*, quite simply, wouldn't have been possible without him. His encouragement, his time, and his love have propelled it forward—as they always do me in every step of my life.

Of course I want to thank my children, Jack and Emmeline, who have read countless books, yet are always yearning and curious for more. They've given feedback on parts of this draft, and plenty of ideas. Right now, Jack's favorite books are the Wingfeather saga, the Prince Warrior series, and the Harry Potter series, but he'll be onto something else tomorrow. Emmeline's favorite books right now are *Wonder, Don't Let the Pigeon Drive the Bus, Madeline,* and *Molly: A Winning Spirit (The American Girl Doll Story)*. It was important for me to publish this book for them, ("their book" as they call it), before either of them finish elementary school. It will be published just in time.

I hope *Wondrous Reading* will prove a gift to many other children who will fall in love with some of the same books my children have at the ages they are now and will pass that love on to many future generations of readers.

I want to thank the University of the Incarnate Word students who have taken my children's literature and Catholicism classes, not only in that one semester, but all who have enthusiastically been a part of my class discussions and creative projects, reminiscing about their childhoods and contemplating their spiritual selves. These students have dreamt and thought through best practices for spiritual reading and teaching along with me for years. One special quality about UIW students is their insatiable desire to discern truth. I hope this book helps those future teachers, religious leaders, and parents in my classes and beyond who have told me they have

Acknowledgments

been yearning for a guide that could help them navigate the specifically Catholic questions they come into my classes seeking answers for, both for themselves and the future children whose lives they will eventually guide.

I absolutely have to thank the Office of Research and Graduate Studies at UIW, particularly Mark Nijland and Lende Bird, who have given me time and breathing room to make this project possible. They are saints in the making at UIW. Every interaction I have with them is filled with God's presence.

I mentioned him above, but I want to thank Tim O'Malley. He probably regrets mentioning the idea for this book in my office, namely because he has inspired me to try hard intellectual and spiritual things—which has led to more bemoaning on my end that he has listened to with the patience of Job well after that day in my office. And yet—at each stage of learning and trying—I've experienced some of the most exciting, fruitful work I've ever accomplished. I'm now doing work that feels as it if it is part of a vocational calling, and it's all because Tim has taken the time to be one of the best friends and mentors I could ever imagine, helping me especially during that pandemic moment when I needed a friend and mentor the most. He is doing God's work in the world on a grand scale, yet he helped me form and bring into fruition this small dream of mine. For that I will always be appreciative.

I also want to thank Artur Sebastian Rosman for letting me publish about children's literature and Catholicism in Notre Dame's *Church Life Journal*. Artur is another ridiculously smart friend who has let me experiment and try things in my writing that I never would have without his encouragement. This book would have remained forever an idea without my having first been published in *Church Life*.

There are colleagues who encourage you to expand, and there are colleagues who understand you better than anyone else. Robin Cadwallader is the latter. She has read and offered feedback on this book from start to finish. I often call her the better part of my brain because her eyes are refined and her logic makes mine better and clearer. She sees where I'm headed, and where I want to and can go. She asks me frankly, and often, why I didn't write what I meant to say in the first place. I am blessed to know her, and I am blessed that she reads my work and offers not only criticism but also comments that show she's engaged in a discussion with my ideas—a rare treasure in the world. She is a providential friend, a gift from God to this Earth and to me. I'm grateful for her beyond measure.

Acknowledgments

Also, I want to thank my parish community at the Annunciation of the Blessed Virgin Mary in St. Hedwig, Texas, who give me spiritual life. Even more specifically, I'd like to thank my parish friends who are a part of my Well-Read Mom reading group, led by Heidi Jones. It is a blessing to talk about literature in general, but especially to talk about children's literature with other smart women and moms invested in the future of the Catholic Church, including through raising, and reading with each other, and with all of our children whom we love while we all "do life" together.

Finally, I want to thank the Holy Spirit for guiding my words in writing this book, as I believe he will your eyes and hearts as you read this book with the children you love.

How to Read This Book

WELCOME TO WONDROUS READING: *Encountering the Catholic Faith in Children's Literature*! As someone who has picked up this book, you likely already know that children's literature, by its very nature, can spark unexpected and fruitful conversations. These conversations can take various forms—from lighthearted and whimsical to educational and profoundly thought-provoking.

Best-known for her Wrinkle in Time Series, renowned Christian children's book author Madeleine L'Engle shares these thoughts on children's literature:

> The writer whose words are going to be read by children has a heavy responsibility. And, yet, despite the undeniable fact that the children's minds are tender, they are also far more tough than people realize, and they have an openness and ability to grapple with difficult concepts which many adults have lost. Writers of children's literature are set apart by their willingness to confront difficult questions.[1]

What L'Engle claims is true in my experience with my own children. Children are tender and sweet, yet they are also open to asking big questions about why the world is as it is: They are naturally curious. My eight-year-old son asks "why" repeatedly every day, so much so that my family jokes about his habit. Why is the sky blue? Why is the Earth round? Why does the family dog bark? He also asks bigger questions: Why do you love me? Why does God love me? Why does God let people die? Often, in the rush of family

---

1. L'Engle, "Dare to Be Creative!"

activities and car rides from this place or that, his questions get lost in the mix, waiting, we tend to say, for a more opportune time to answer them.

When we sit down to read together, this opportune time naturally comes because we're choosing as a family to make space for it. L'Engle states that the writer of children's literature bears a heavy responsibility, but the reader of children's literature does, too. When we read with children, we delve into their imaginations together, letting the questions they might have about the world flow. Just as writers of children's literature are set apart by their willingness to confront difficult questions, guardians of children's souls ought to consider themselves set apart in this way.

The question naturally beget is: How do we confront difficult questions with children we love? In reading together, we enter a rare, wondrous space wherein children's questions merge with an openness to soul searching, an openness on the part of adult and child reader alike. Answering faith questions when reading does not engender the same feeling or response as addressing doctrine during a prescribed catechetical time and hour dictated by one's parish. The difficult questions crop up naturally. The seeking and openness to discovering spiritual answers happens often via selfless curiosity about events and happenings in characters' lives other than our own. In being curious about others' experiences, truths about one's own are often unveiled.

As Catholic readers, we have a specific responsibility when reading that goes beyond building empathy or teaching universal values. We are not only shepherds of our children's physical and emotional selves, but also of their spiritual ones. Children's literature is one way we have to cultivate children's wonder, or natural curiosity, about the world they live in, wonder about God and life's greater meaning.

Reading is a tool we have in our Catholic spiritual toolbox, then. Through reading, we have the opportunity to pause, pray, and reflect on our faith together, ensuring that we make the time to ponder life's bigger questions. This book is your companion to explore and deepen your understanding of the Catholic faith alongside reading to and with the children you love. It offers insights and discussion points for parents, educators, church leaders, and other book lovers to navigate meaningful conversations with children.

Engaging with the Chapters

This book has five chapters—an introductory chapter about the book's purpose and four thematic chapters that focus on a unique Catholic theme.

In each of the four thematic chapters, we'll explore a Catholic concept through the lens of one picture book and one chapter book. Topics you will find include the benefits of living liturgically, the interplay of faith and reason, the fostering of a culture of life, and the care and nurturing of God's creation. As you delve into each of these chapters, consider the following four steps:

1. **Choose Books That Match Your Child's Maturity Level**

   Each thematic chapter will provide an analysis of a picture book and a chapter book that relate to that chapter's theme. I'll share the generally recommended age ranges for each book based on recommendations from publishers and educators. However, it's essential to trust your understanding of your children's maturity levels because, as you have likely experienced, individual children's maturity levels vary. Finally, discussing significant topics can be more comfortable and accessible when using books as launching pads, even if they don't necessarily match the commonly associated age ranges for that book. It's not uncommon for picture books to captivate teenagers just as effectively as elementary school children and vice versa. Use your own discernment as a guide.

2. **Create Sacred Reading Time**

   Carve out intentional moments for family or group reading by designating a cozy and quiet space that fosters reflection—perhaps a charming book nook nestled in a corner of a bedroom or a classroom. However, don't feel confined by the pursuit of perfection. My children and I often listen to audiobooks or read print books aloud during car rides to and from gymnastics practice, while running errands, or traveling on road trips. Our cars and backpacks are filled with books tucked into pockets, ready for those moments when we find ourselves waiting in line at doctors' offices or hair appointments. While a dedicated space at home is wonderful and comforting, remember that reading—and learning—can unfold anywhere, at any time. The key is simply to ensure that you make reading a habit however it fits your lifestyle or organizational structure, whether the reading is planned or serendipitous. One way to make any reading time sacred, no matter where you are, is to offer a brief prayer to God before starting. Your prayer can be as simple as this:

Dear God,
Bless our reading moments.
Grant us joy, inspiration, and discovery.
Help us to read with your divine purpose in mind.
In the Name of the Father, the Son, and the Holy Spirit,
Amen.

3. **Let Questions and Activities Flow**

Children, with their natural curiosity, often have big questions about the world. As you read together, encourage them to ask questions and to explore their ideas through imagination. Lean into what interests your child-readers. At the end of each thematic chapter, you'll also find questions as resources you can use with children to foster deeper reflection about the books included and the chapter's focus. After each question is a suggested activity you can do to engage children's minds further. Plus, you'll find an appendix at the end of this book with additional text suggestions aligned with each chapter's topic, as well as a question related to each book that can help inspire faith-filled interpretations of it. Reading, like going to Mass, is not a solitary activity; it is an opportunity for communal exploration. The questions provided at the end of each chapter and in the appendix are designed to prompt dialogue, to encourage you to share your thoughts, listen to the perspectives of the children in your care, and build engagement and close relationships.

A Living Document

What I'm hoping you will find most in each chapter is inspiration. Reading with children provides a habit that you can cultivate, one that will help you to explore your Catholic faith in reflective and interactive ways that work for your family, school, or parish. In *The Read-Aloud Family: Making Meaningful and Lasting Connections with Your Kids*, Sarah Mackenzie, a homeschooling mother and popular podcaster, writes, "The stories we read together act as a bridge when we can't seem to find some other way to connect. They are our currency, our language, our family culture. The words

How to Read This Book

and stories we share become part of our family identity."[2] If your family identity is Catholic, as mine is, use reading together to contemplate your family's faith life. Make your faith part of your reading culture, in whatever way this book can serve your goals. It might not be second nature to you yet, but it's worth the practice and the transformational impact it can have. You can start with this book's introduction about how reading together can transform your faith life, or you can start with the first thematic chapter exploring liturgical living. You may also save that chapter for later and start with another thematic chapter about a particular topic you're especially interested in or that covers a beloved book you spotted in the table of contents. The goal of *Wondrous Reading* is to help you embrace the profound impact literature can have on your family, school, or parish. Read and use it, however, and in whatever order, you'd like, keeping in mind its intended aim to strengthen children's relationships with loved ones, evoke spiritual contemplation, and forge lasting memories centered around reading experiences.

One suggestion I have about the thematic chapters is to read aloud the analysis sections I've written about certain books *after* you and your loved ones have read the book together. If you'd prefer, you can even read the suggested books independently, each member of your family or other group finding reading time that works for your respective schedules. Then, you can gather for a monthly book club, reading the chapter's analysis section and delving into the questions and activities. With the picture books suggested, you can even read them moments before meeting to discuss them. However hectic your life is, this book, and the readings and discussions it suggests, can fit within it. I even have a group of families within my parish with whom I read picture and chapter books alike, depending on our collective schedules. This keeps us accountable and broadens our reading community.

As you read my analysis of the books included in the following chapters, either silently or aloud, see if you agree or disagree with what my family and our reading culture has found as significant within the texts. What other books might your family add that fit a particular chapter's theme? What other topics or questions might you add to the list provided at the end of a chapter? In other words, how are you inspired to move beyond the book's scope and content?

---

2. Mackenzie, *Read-Aloud Family*.

Wondrous Reading

In incorporating your Catholic faith into your reading culture, you set out on a sacred adventure—a journey of exploration and contemplation that I hope enriches your family, school, or local parish identity and its relationship with the universal Church. When practicing reading with your Catholic faith at the center, I hope you discover how the power of stories can shape and deepen your spiritual journey. By undertaking a shared literary exploration, you not only cultivate a habit of reading but also nurture a space for meaningful conversations that can bond you and develop your spiritual acumen, independently and as a family or child-centered reading group. Cherish these moments, recognizing that through the gift of literature, you're building a legacy of faith, love, and understanding—a legacy poised to endure and inspire generations of faithful Catholics, now and in the future.

Introduction

Reading for the Soul:
Growing in Faith Through Children's Literature

"When we pray we speak to God; but when
we read, God speaks to us."

ST. JEROME

REMEMBER, FOR A MOMENT, being read to as a child. Most of us can recall a reading experience with someone else when we were younger. Who was it that read to you? A parent? A teacher? A librarian? Someone else? Recall where you were. What did the space look like? What did it smell like? Were you next to someone? Were you sitting in their lap or nestled up next to them? Or, were you sitting in a group, maybe in a circle on brightly colored rectangular mats? Or, were you lying in a bed at night, reading with a flashlight or perhaps via the light emanating from the crack in a closet door on the other side of the room?

Take a moment to recall the story of the book. What happened in it? Were there monsters, dragons, princesses, or perhaps ordinary children exhibiting extraordinary feats of courage? What did the book look like? Maybe you can recall its cover or the pictures inside it, if you are remembering a book from early or middle childhood. When speaking to a friend recently, I listened as she recalled that the girl character on the cover of her favorite children's book wore a bright red coat and that the book smelled musty; she recalled turning the pages, which felt brittle, and she worried they might break beneath her touch. Similarly, in my memories, some of the books scattered throughout my house were bound by covers from a century before, covers that had once been hard but had since become soft and textured, feeling like worn fabric to the touch. Their muted cover colors of blue, green, or burgundy recalled the rich vibrancy of their past intense pigmentation.

Other books I encountered as a child were shiny, glossy, bright, and new: Pictures of babies and animals paraded over their pages. I remember eagerly awaiting what would happen next in a story I had read one thousand times prior, laughing as a beloved character would appear again or gasping in renewed glee at a "surprise" plot twist that I had begun to look forward to in rereading—the twist now a comfort of sorts, a prior knowing of what was to occur next and being in on the secret, so to speak. *The Cat in the Hat* and *If You Give a Mouse a Cookie* are examples of these book memories for me.

Recall, now, if you can for a moment, how reading one of your favorite books made you *feel* as a child. Lean into the feelings the memory gives you now, in this moment. You might feel comfort, joy, sadness, silliness, or a mix of all these emotions. *The Velveteen Rabbit* summons an entirely different feeling than *Treasure Island*, for instance. Nostalgia, from one, adventure from the other. *The Bridge to Terabithia* still tugs at my heart. As a professor of children's literature, I often discuss favorite childhood books with young adults in college, and they almost always bring up this novel—the memory of the grief responses the novel evoked etched in their hearts. Often, these eighteen- to twenty-two-year-olds will laugh with nervous embarrassment at the novel's mere mention and the bubbling of feeling that speaking of it draws them into; other times, they pause with recognition at its name, become starkly serious when they say it, repeating the title in a whisper: We suddenly enter hallowed territory together. Have you read it too?, they inquire. When I nod, knowingly, they express deep-seated feelings of camaraderie. We know each other; we share in each other's lives, in this moment.

Reading experiences, especially those involving children's and young adult literature, can make us feel a range of emotions, often dependent on the books, the people, and the environments in which we encountered the stories, but almost always, they make us *feel*. Because children's and young adult books bring us into an awareness of some of life's biggest questions and experiences—and can help us to cope with the emotions we already bring to the table—we cling to those books and the memories they instill in us long after the ending is announced, recalling them later as sacred

Introduction

moments that our adult reading enterprises can never quite seem to imitate. When we read books as children, those books become part of our learning journeys as scholars and as humans trying to think through the meaning behind why we exist in this world and how we ought to try to forge relationships with others—and perhaps, too, how we ought to try to forge a relationship with the God who created us and formed us into relational beings in the first place.

This book is about deepening an understanding and feeling of Catholic faith through the study of literature, both your own and that of the children and young adults whom you love, through developing and encouraging reading practices that delve into faith inquiry. Whether you are a parent, an educator, a religious education teacher, a member of the clergy, a ministry worker, or an academic like me who studies children's and young adult literature—or literature and/or theology more generally—this book is for you. There is great benefit in exploring how reading as a dedicated practice can serve as a path to teach and inspire faith.

Reading, as a practice, takes children and adults to a different place—together. It invites them to forget themselves and to imagine the experiences of another and each other—adult and child—deeply and thoroughly. With the right questions, intentionality, and spirit, adults reading with children can help them to discuss and to feel God as a constant part of their lives and communities, inclusive with and helpful to attending Mass, partaking in the sacraments, and participating in specific religious events. Adding reading as another practice for faith formation embeds into the fabric of children's lives questions of human nature and God throughout each and every week, acting as a constant appendage of and support for the other important rituals of the Catholic Church.

Reading literature of all kinds—canonical and noncanonical, Catholic-centered or not—offers a unique opportunity to help guide children and young adults as they explore and hopefully refine and deepen their religious selves. Reading aloud with children can be one mechanism to help a faith life grow stronger because it encourages children simultaneously to trust and to build relationships with educators, parents, and caretakers. It also allows them space to ask difficult questions when some children otherwise might keep those queries to themselves, afraid perhaps that asking a question might upset those they love. Other children perhaps simply might not have enough targeted, deep spaces of time in which asking theological and emotional questions feels natural with the adults who care about their spiritual lives. This book suggests that adding imaginative reading as part of a Catholic child's religious practice provides room for spiritual and moral conversations that can lead readers of all ages, children and adults alike, to a more robust religious life, communally and independently.

Certainly, it is an apt time for those who care about Catholic children and the future of the Church to begin to consider new modes of reviving and energizing children's faith lives and their understanding of religion. In 2016, a study was released that revealed young adults are leaving, or disaffiliating from, the Catholic Church in alarmingly high numbers. The Center for Applied Research in the Apostolate (CARA), in conjunction with St. Mary's Press, found that "[a]pproximately 12.8 percent of young adults in the U.S. between 18 and 25 are former Catholics, and that approximately 6.8 percent of U.S. teens between the ages of 15 and 17 are former Catholics."[1] Perhaps most striking is that children are leaving "as early as age 10, with the median age of 13."[2]

As a reference point, you might note that some of the most well-known stand-alone classic books for children in the ten to thirteen age range are *Peter Pan; Roll of Thunder, Hear My Cry;* and *Charlotte's Web*. Christian series classics that also fall into this category are The Chronicles of Narnia, Anne of Green Gables, and The Lord of the Rings. Recall now, if you might, yourself at age ten, skipping rope perhaps. Riding a bike. Hula hooping. Swinging. Imagine making the decision *at age ten* to leave your childhood faith. According to disaffiliation research, these children are already feeling injured by the Church and are making the decision to leave because their caretakers or those within the Church itself have hurt them, or they are drifting away from Catholicism because of a lack of community, or they might be leaving because they dissent from the Church's prevailing doctrines (intriguingly, the study indicates children often don't fully comprehend the doctrines they disagree with, a failing of catechesis). Indeed, these are the three primary reasons young people cite as precipitating their decisions to leave the faith.

I suggest, perhaps radically, that maintaining a sustained, habitual reading practice with a child or young adult could address each and every one of these reasons. One participant in the CARA study, "Amy," reported, "When I reflect back, I think my initial doubts began with my childhood diabetes. I would always ask, 'Why me? Why would God do this to

---

1. McCarty and Vitek, *Going, Going, Gone*, 5.
2. McCarty and Vitek, *Going, Going, Gone*, 6.

Introduction

somebody? Why would he let something like that happen to somebody who has been going to church religiously?"[3] Difficult questions of grief and suffering are certainly found at the heart of the Christian story of Christ's death and resurrection, and you might have felt, as I did, an immediate desire to comfort Amy with doctrinal truths. However, Amy's dissatisfaction comes from the heart, stems from her personal experience, and it is one perhaps that a discussion of doctrine alone could not solve. Possibly another approach would be to engage her heart and her mind through the power of narrative, as Jesus did in the parables.

Here, I bring in an example from *Esperanza Rising*, a popular contemporary children's book targeted to ages nine through fourteen. It is a story that I've taught and that my son, a third grader, recently read in his public school. The eponymous character in the novel, Esperanza, reflects at the narrative's end on her life having not gone according to plan and the suffering with which it has been filled. She has been forced to immigrate from Mexico to California, has dealt with the grief of her father's murder, and has gone from wealthy to poor during the Great Depression—yet she still manages to find meaning in her existence. She says to her friend Miguel, as they gaze at a vineyard in California, "See these perfect rows, Miguel? They are like what my life would have been. These rows know where they are going. Straight ahead. Now my life is like the zigzag in the blanket on Mama's bed."[4]

Esperanza dreams of bringing her ailing *abuelita* from Mexico and being reunited with her. When talking to Miguel, she finds connection with her Catholic family, and she realizes that she does not control where her life goes. Of course, there isn't a perfect analogy here for Amy's situation who recounts that her struggles with diabetes first pushed her away from the faith, but this could be a teachable moment. Were Amy reading *Esperanza Rising* with an adult who cared about her faith formation, they could have talked about the Catholic Social Teaching regarding human dignity. Both the real-life Amy and the fictional Esperanza are image-bearers of God, after all, one might say. Humans are all meant to need each other, to live with and alongside one another, like the "zigzag[s]" in Esperanza's "mama's blanket," just as Amy needs others because of her diabetes (and likely as she would help others, if someone were to ask her).

---

3. McCarty and Vitek, *Going, Going, Gone*, 25.
4. Muñoz Ryan, *Esperanza Rising*, 224.

God is relational—the Father, Son, and Holy Spirit: Indeed, from a Catholic understanding, all of our lives are relational. When we are thrown off course, we learn the mercy of others toward us, and if that mercy isn't shown toward us—if we are left alone when we need mercy—the mere fact that it is missing from our lives helps us to remember that we can make the world better by showing it to others. We can be image-bearers of God for others and remind them that they are image-bearers, too. Together, relationally, then, we can build Christ's kingdom on Earth. We can make our world better, much as Esperanza in the novel aspires to do as she dreams of bringing her *abuelita* to California.

This is a quick look at one moment in *Esperanza Rising*, but it indicates how reading with children can provide opportunities to discuss questions they may have about Catholicism and God in a setting that doesn't seem as intimidating as a formal religious education class. This doesn't mean that reading with children will always bring up these types of in-depth questions. But, ideally, reading will build a trusting relationship, so the child you're reading with feels comfortable asking any range of questions as they arise. Significantly, purposefully, and thoughtfully engaging with all types of questions, small and large, has the potential to be transformational in the faith lives of readers of all ages.

With this said, educators, caretakers, guardians, and parents—that is, anyone who is engaging in reading as a faith practice with children—shouldn't feel obligated to know every facet of the Catholic Church's teaching or feel that when a question is brought up, they must immediately know its answer. As a Catholic convert, I certainly do not know everything and often feel behind regarding the ins and outs of Church teaching. I am aware, however—perhaps precisely because of this constant feeling that I am behind—that humility is the first virtue of the faith. Thus, when I don't know the answers to my children's or my young adult college students' faith or theology questions, I'm honest with them. Then, I take the time to investigate what the Church teaches and talk about it when I have located an answer; perhaps I find it right away, or perhaps it takes a while and we have to come back to it during our next reading or class session. Importantly, with adolescent and young adult readers, I always relay what I've found and then let them reflect and discuss it, providing a venue in which there's an openness to disagreement, dialogue, and long-term discernment.

Proceeding this way, I ensure that when they have questions, they know they can continue to come to the table with them, and we can wrestle

Introduction

with them together, over time; when reading is a ritual, there's space to revisit big questions—and big emotions. A blessing of being a convert is that I didn't convert overnight. I remember, and know, conversion of the heart and mind takes time. I struggled with many of the Church's teachings. Therefore, I want to invite the discussions and give the faith—and God—time to build relationship through reading, dialogue, contemplation, ritual, and prayer.

When we read with children and young adults, the relationships we construct with them are *reciprocal* and *communal.* That is, the relationships are built on back-and-forth engagement between adults and young readers and also on back-and-forth engagement between God and adult and young readers alike. Remembering God's centrality, and to trust in his plan for our cognitive, social, and spiritual development, is essential to treating imaginative reading as a faith practice. Just as having children has taught me much about the world, including everything from potty training to language acquisition, it has also taught me about the love of God and, by extension, about the Church and its doctrines. More than anything else, though, parenting, and my relationship with my children, has humbled me in every aspect, grounding me in that virtue of humility.

In *Laudato Si'*, Pope Francis writes, "Once we lose our humility, and become enthralled with the possibility of limitless mastery over everything, we inevitably end up harming society and the environment."[5] I see the reading practices I've built within my family life and in my classroom spaces as integral ecologies in and of themselves: They are microcosms of Francis's holistic vision of the relationships we have on this Earth. These integral relationships, both in my family and my classroom, affect the world at large. Further, my personal, distinct, and different place in each of these ecological spaces must be undertaken with humility, as yours should be in whatever realm you find yourself when you're reading with young people. To state it differently, when reading with children and young adults with the Catholic faith at the center, we simply need to be aspirational, loving, and habitual—not perfect. Our children and young adults don't need perfection. They need encounter and love.

Indeed, reading together, and loving those with whom we're reading, is akin to prayer, to how we speak our love as humans to God, when it is practiced continually. When we read with children and young adults, we show our love to them and communicate with them. If we do so with a faith-oriented

---

5. Francis, *Laudato Si'*, sec. 224.

perspective, as this book proposes, we keep God at the center of our intentional practices with youth, wherever they might occur. Matthew 22:37–39, which is often heralded as the bedrock of the Christian faith, reads as follows: "Jesus replied: 'Love the Lord your God with all your heart and with all your soul and with all your mind.' This is the first and greatest commandment. And the second is like it: 'Love your neighbor as yourself.'"[6]

Significantly, reading stories has children and adults alike pause everything they are doing and spend time in dedicated contemplation of someone who is traveling a path different from theirs. That is, reading is an open invitation to "love your neighbor as yourself." Children and young adults who read spend time considering others constantly. We always have the option to pray with young people before reading, to ask that our reading is geared toward God. In and of itself, though, reading can be interpreted as an extension of a type of contemplative life. It strengthens those muscles needed for a strong prayer life because, when we read, we meditate and reflect on others for a long period of time, pausing that ever constant focus on self. *When we read, we are present in a moment.* We move from an inward gaze, locked in on our thoughts and our feelings, to an outward gaze, where we begin to consider the thoughts and feelings of others. In his "Catechesis on Prayer," given in the Library of the Apostolic Palace in 2021, Pope Francis explains, "To pray for others is the first way to love them."[7] Reading with children and young adults provides an entrée into this type of self-forgetting love.

Indeed, reading from this perspective is one of the best ways to teach children how to pray. When children read, they are immersed in a story. They are meditating on a single idea, and they are swept away in the narrative; their thoughts are captured by nothing but the story—and ours are, too, if we are reading alongside them. Community and independent reading alike foster a meditative experience, wherein children learn that words bring power and that we can imagine and consider new ways of thinking about the world together. *The Catechism of the Catholic Church* points out that prayer is "God's Gift." It is "the raising of one's mind and heart to God."[8] For anyone who has had young children or who has been around them

---

6. All biblical references in this book will be taken from the New International Version.

7. Francis, "Catechesis on Prayer," para. 7.

8. Catholic Church, *Catechism*, no. 2559.

Introduction

for any period of time, it is hard to imagine them focused on anyone but themselves and their most immediate needs.

They know when they need to eat, drink, play, and sleep—and perhaps throw some fits in the middle if they're not getting their needs met. That is, they are mainly focused on lower-order, physical concerns. Swiss psychologist Jean Piaget calls toddler through age seven the preoperational stage. This stage is self-centered, but it is ripe with imaginative impulses. From ages seven through ten, children reach the concrete operational stage. At this stage, they are increasingly aware of the world externally, and they begin to realize that their thoughts may not be shared by everyone.[9] Reading, as an art form, takes young children outside of themselves and helps them to imagine another space, another way of being and viewing the world.

Practicing this, and keeping to it, from an early age prepares children for a strong prayer life as they progress into middle and young adulthood—and hopefully beyond. Further, as adults read with children, they benefit from the meditative practices that reading forms. In an opinion piece published in *The New Yorker* about how reading can lead to a life of happiness, South African writer Ceridwen Dovey shares, "Reading has been shown to put our brains into a pleasurable trance-like state, similar to meditation, and it brings the same health benefits of deep relaxation and inner calm. Regular readers sleep better, have lower stress levels, higher self-esteem, and lower rates of depression than non-readers."[10]

Consider how reading can benefit the inner emotional life and then consider these facts from the Center for Disease Control about anxiety and depression being consistently on the rise among US children. Both mental conditions increased in children ages "6–17 years . . . from 5.4% in 2003 to 8% in 2007 and to 8.4% in 2011–2012."[11] In 2019, 15.1 percent of children from ages twelve to seventeen reported "a major depressive episode" and "18.8% seriously contemplated suicide."[12] If reading can lead us to happier, calmer, more meditative lives, it may be worth honing as a habitual practice to help guide youth and adults alike to healthier, holistic mindsets. For Catholic parents, educators, and ministers, a holistic mindset will entail components of spiritual practice and formation. Psychologists suggest in the journal *Cognition and Emotion* that narrative fiction in particular, as opposed to nonfiction

---

9. Ansorge, "Piaget's Stages of Development."
10. Dovey, "Can Reading Make You Happier?," para. 15.
11. Children's Lifetime, "Data and Statistics on Children's Mental Health," para. 8.
12. Children's Lifetime, "Data and Statistics on Children's Mental Health," para. 8.

and other art forms, moves readers emotionally and that "[o]nce one has finished reading, these emotions don't simply dissipate but may have an impact that lasts hours or days, long after closing the covers of the book, perhaps reemerging whenever the book is brought to mind."[13]

These psychologists cite a study in which a control group of participants were asked to read Anton Chekhov's short story "The Lady with the Toy Dog," while another group was provided a similar amount of reading in scope and length but not of the same artistic quality. Those who read the short story were not only emotionally moved in a way the other group was not, but they also perceived their personality differently after completing the reading.[14] That is, their senses of self were changed because of reading literature. They didn't simply *feel* something about the reading material; they also *viewed themselves* differently. Note that this study represents *one* controlled inquiry conducted in *one* time and place. Imagine the potential that reading narrative fiction could have on the hearts and minds of children if families and educators were to make it part and parcel of religious practice and discussion.

In *Desiring the Kingdom: Worship, Worldview, and Cultural Formation*, James K. A. Smith makes the case that the habits we foster create our sense of identity. These habits are based in what we desire, or love. As humans, we are "always ultimately aimed at *a telos*, a picture of the good life that pulls us toward it, thus shaping our actions and behavior."[15] The habits that form our identity the most he dubs "thick," or "meaning-full. . . . Engaging in these habit-forming practices not only says something about us, but also keeps shaping us into [those] kind of [people]."[16] In other words, the more often we engage in a thick activity, the more we become the type of people who are identified by that practice. Not all thick habits are necessarily religious, but they are all identity-formational in some way, according to Smith. Reading as a practice is one activity I would identify as a "thick" habit in the way that Smith defines it, especially during the time span when children are learning to read (generally ages zero to five), though the transformational nature of the behavior drops off the older a child becomes. As a family practice, reading together drops off as a child ages. Utility increasingly overtakes the wonder, the meditative practice, and the discussion that reading can

---

13. Mar et al., "Emotion and Narrative Fiction," 818.
14. Mar et al., "Emotion and Narrative Fiction," 829.
15. Smith, *Desiring the Kingdom*, 80.
16. Smith, *Desiring the Kingdom*, 82.

Introduction

bring to children and adults alike. Indeed, in schools we see this drop-off too. Communal and independent reading practices cease for utility's sake. When children reach the higher grades of elementary school and beyond, they generally are reading textbooks in lieu of literature as ways of learning and knowing.

And rather than reading aloud or silently during class, "[c]hildren are required to respond to computerized tests about books they have read"[17] outside of class, and national standardized testing on reading becomes the norm. In 2016, a national study conducted by Scholastic indicated that only 17 percent of children were still read to by the age of nine.[18] It was not children, however, who wished their parents would stop reading; it seems as if the stopping of reading together is an imaginary marker of adulthood that caretakers impose upon youth, not the other way around. Indeed, 87 percent of children surveyed between the ages of six and eleven said that they enjoyed being read to by their parents and wished their parents would continue the practice.[19] In that same study, Scholastic reveals that "the percentage of parents reading aloud to their children after the age of five drops significantly. By the age of eleven, very few children are hearing a book read aloud."[20]

Notice the psychological and emotional transition that takes place for children and parents. Reading, which for young children is a time of bonding and togetherness, becomes relegated to a task that must be completed, an assignment to be graded. It no longer feels meaning-full but more like a chore, or part of a to-do list. Acclaimed children's author Beverly Cleary has articulated that "[c]hildren should learn that reading is for pleasure, not just something teachers make you do in school."[21] When we make reading a chore, we rob children of the pleasure that reading used to and should continue to give them. Imaginative reading is one of the best modes to reach young people's hearts, yet we have collectively decided as adults to create an arbitrary cut-off for fostering pleasure-filled reading practices, likely because we believe children no longer want or need shared reading time. If we are already school educators, we ought to reconsider how we're teaching the art of reading. Are we teaching it in ways that rob children of the joy and emotional and spiritual import it can have? This line of questioning is

---

17. Trelease, *Read-Aloud Handbook*, 11.
18. Scholastic, "Kids and Family Reading Report," 201.
19. Scholastic, "Kids and Family Reading Report," 201.
20. Trelease, *Read-Aloud Handbook*, 37.
21. Quoted in Wink, *Power of Story*, 7.

not to say that all schools and teachers are alike in how they teach reading. I suggest here that parents, guardians, and educators all have an opportunity to assess anew how they can be examples to the children they love about creating pleasurable reading habits that can lead to impactful, emotional, and spiritual formation.

Ideally, reading experiences ought to be communal as much as possible. They should build community, and they shouldn't stop after elementary school, not simply because children themselves desire for them to continue either. In Jim Trelease's foundational *Read-Aloud Handbook* (first published in 1979 and most recently updated in 2019), educational researchers point out that "reading and listening skills begin to converge at eighth grade. Until then, kids usually listen on a higher level than they read."[22] In other words, children up to fourteen years of age can understand material being read to them at much higher levels than they can reading it for themselves, independently. If we limit children fourteen and younger to books only in their age range, and stop reading aloud to them in elementary school (or even before they leave elementary school), higher levels of narrative inquiry are shut down. Connecting this theory to how we understand and consider deep religious and theological questions, we should consider what is closed off from discussion—what children might be able to enjoy, grapple with, and contemplate—what is taken away from them if they are reading only by themselves.

Now imagine what "thick habits" are replacing time and thoughtfulness in this era of social media and the Internet. Communion with each other, with family, with narratives of life and love are being replaced with consumerism, messages from marketers and celebrities, those desiring not "the good life" for children but a life where children can buy and consume more products. In participating in the madness of the electronic world, we relegate the development of our children's thick cultural habits to others—those who care far less about the children's spiritual journeys than we do. Sarah Mackenzie astutely points out in *The Read-Aloud Family* that reading with a child, and guiding that child's reading, can lead to higher virtue in ways that are difficult to mimic through any other venue. She eloquently asserts, "When it comes to imparting truth to our kids, nagging lectures from an adult simply can't compare with a story whose time has come. A story meets a child where he is. It sparks an authentic desire."[23] Reading

22. Trelease, *Read-Aloud Handbook*, 35.
23. Mackenzie, *Read-Aloud Family*, 49.

forms our identities, ours and our children's, if we let it, and as adults who care about children, we can help to form those identities toward God.

My shifting relationship with literature has certainly helped to shape, and to transform, my identity, especially as I have made reading aloud a habit in my family's home life. For instance, as a parent, I have come to associate certain children's books not only with the reading experiences I had with those books as a child but also with the reading experiences I am currently having with them as a parent to a child. Not only do I understand my seven-year-old daughter and eight-year-old son better because of how they respond to the books we read together as a family, but I also see how my thoughts and emotions differ from theirs.

Reading is spiritually and emotionally transformational for all of us. When we revisit classics, or even books that aren't classics that I once read as a child and want to share with my children, I often respond differently and notice new ideas in them. My children almost always want to know what I thought about a book we're reading when I was a child, if it is one I've encountered in the past. Other questions they often ask run along the lines of, "Who read these books to you? When? Did you like them?" Their questions about my reading experiences in the past, as well as our new experiences of reading books together now, help to form who they are, as reading continues to form who I am and who I am becoming. As aforementioned, reading practices are part of the ecology of our family, an ecology that goes out into the world and hopefully changes it. I learn about myself, my children, and my family because of how we respond, and act upon, the books we read together, a topic I'll explore throughout this book.

Reading as a family has strengthened and deepened my marriage, in addition to my relationship with my children. My husband's reading preferences often differ from mine, and it is a joy for us as parents, and partners, to share books that held value for us as children or that we're choosing to discover newly together and introduce to our family. Our children, and we parents, witness each other encountering emotional reading experiences. For instance, as a children's literature scholar, my primary field of research inquiry is girls' literature of the nineteenth century. Yet, I never read The Little House on the Prairie series books growing up. They were one of the series that my husband's family cherished in their household, though. Reading the series together with our children, and hearing my husband's stories about his first experiences with these books—and how his thoughts on them now have grown and deepened in a second adult reading—has made our family experience with reading those books particularly resonant. Moreover, my husband and I talk about the books we read as a family on a different level with each other than with the children, including how to confront and discuss various topics brought up in the books we read together. Taking time to read as a family has the potential to transform relationships, no matter what the structure of a family may be.

In an April 2022 Plenary Session of the Pontifical Academy of Social Sciences, Pope Francis declared, "The family humanizes people through the relationship of 'we' and at the same time promotes each person's legitimate differences."[24] Reading together builds that "we." It builds the commonality of spending directed, present time with each other, not simply being in the same room or house, but being active together in the same storied thought. It helps us to find and to discover our differences as a family, too, to discuss those differences through narrative what ifs, all while we're still feeling as if we're communally part of a larger story that we're building together. Now that my family has read so much together, we will often reference books as part of building our "we." Reading is part of our family fabric in the large and small parts of life.

The other day, when my daughter put her hand near the oven to try to take out a French fry early, my son jested that she was making a dangerous choice like Annie from the Magic Tree House series does to touch dinosaurs randomly. Likewise, when my son recently whined about wanting to play a video game rather than go outside, my daughter said, "He's crying like Colin" from *The Secret Garden*. Reading builds communities, it forms identities, and it has us feel in ways that most other educational and entertainment platforms simply do not.

Too often, though, families and parishes alike relegate reading, and all discussions about it, to schoolteachers and schoolrooms, eliminating the potential for reading as a faith practice. Principally, it ought to be mentioned that in schools it is often unclear how to talk about and to incorporate religion and faith into classroom discussions in substantive ways, no matter the type of school a child attends. Thus, not only does school often take away the pleasure of reading because of the emphasis on testing, but it also rarely elevates religious or faith discussions as a part of literary study. In public schools, which account for the educational facilities of 90 percent of US students, "There seems to be ongoing confusion about what teachers can say and do . . . when it comes to religion. Adding to the dilemma is the

---

24. Vatican News, "Rediscover the Value of Human Life," para. 8.

Introduction

ongoing debate regarding how to navigate issues of religious freedom and expression within" such facilities.[25] Further, "[m]ost colleges of education are sending graduates into public school classrooms who have never been taught about religious freedom or how it and the First Amendment apply to public schools."[26]

Pre-service teachers across the board, whether they are teaching in religious schools or public schools, are generally well versed in discussing issues of race, class, gender, and other frameworks of intersectional identity markers and experiences when it comes to analyzing and considering literature. Most of them, though, are never required to take a religion class as part of their teacher education training; plus, in religion classes, were they to take one, ways to discuss literature and faith in their future classrooms are not addressed. Stated simply, most teachers are not provided targeted instruction on how to address religion in novels, short stories, and poetry.

In public schools especially, if teachers are confused or worried about what they can discuss legally with students, it makes sense that once they are in their classrooms, they would simply opt to choose other facets of literature to attend to besides religion or faith. Students may be allowed to talk about their faith practices, but it seems unlikely they will if their teachers don't initiate such discussions. And why would most teachers risk their careers by bringing faith discussions into their classrooms? Consider how often public school board meetings have been in the news recently because of questions about the content being taught in classrooms, and consider the legal cases being brought up over whether and what facets of religion can and cannot be taught in public schools. In the same vein, if religion isn't a facet of identity that's brought up in discussions of literature in teacher education classes, then teachers won't be as equipped to test students on it, even as an academic subject.

How often can you remember faith practices of characters or even the religious experiences students felt while reading a text, both of which are allowable constitutional principles for teachers and students, being discussed in school? Beyond the permissibility of such discussions, however, faith is part and parcel of many children's lives, and religious experiences have informed and been embedded in stories since the first narratives were ever conceived. No matter whether a student is attending a public or a private school,

---

25. Hartwick and Logan, "Teaching and Talking about Religion," 171.
26. Hartwick and Logan, "Teaching and Talking about Religion," 168.

though, most teachers are not given training in how to talk about religion and literature thoughtfully with their students.

If they never discuss with adults the ways faith is developed, articulated, and grappled with in narrative form, children lose out during their most formative years. If stories emotionally move children and adults, they offer an avenue toward deeper intellectual and spiritual understanding of faith and the nuances that have shaped literature for generations and into the present day. It is not only children who lose such deep opportunities for growth and development, though. Educators, academics, parents, ministry workers, caretakers of all kinds, and those who consider themselves to be seekers of truth will be stalled in this part of their development. As this introduction has attempted to argue, reading literature is one of the most emotionally motivating ways for children to encounter faith experiences and to contemplate how others have similarly undergone heartening and challenging journeys about the ways in which religion intersects the other aspects of their lives.

Andrew Greeley states it this way in his foundational book on *The Catholic Imagination*: "Cognitive psychologists have recently begun to insist that metaphors—statements that one reality is like another reality—are the fundamental tools of human knowledge. We understand better and explain more adequately one reality to ourselves by comparing it to another reality we already know."[27] Literature helps children to compare their individual worlds with those of others, to compare their faiths and emotional lives to someone else's, and to delve into the deep, hard questions these comparisons generate. Parents can begin by asking their children what they're reading at school as a matter of analogy. Even better, though, parents and religious educators of all kinds can build reading communities open to thoughtful inquiries of faith.

Imagine, then, the changes that could be made to students' faith lives when emotion meets doctrine. Consider what questions might be asked if, when reading stories together, adults and children took seriously the faith lives of the characters they encounter inside those stories and by proxy took seriously their own faith lives. How might parents and educators harness the power of literature for children and young adults to help Catholic faith communities become stronger, in dialogue, emotion, conviction, and, most important, in love?

---

27. Greeley, *Catholic Imagination*, 6.

Introduction

This book contains four chapters, which explore different aspects of the Catholic faith and how these are addressed in canonical or popular children's literature. Each of these chapters explores one shorter, or picture, book and one longer, or chapter, book that presents the issues addressed. At the conclusion of each chapter, there is a set of age-appropriate questions that can be used to guide discussions and some related activity ideas. There is also a robust appendix with a list of other children's book titles for "suggested reading" about the faith topics as well as broad questions that might be used for children and young adults as you read this or other literature with faith formation in mind.

The topics you will find in *Wondrous Reading* include the benefits of living liturgically, explored through *The Giving Tree* and *Cecilia's Magical Mission*; the assessment of the compatibility of faith and reason, explored through *Goodnight Moon* and the Magic Tree House series; the fostering of a culture of life, explored through *Alma and How She Got Her Name* and *Little Women*; and the care and nurturing of God's creation, explored through *The Snowy Day* and *The Wind in the Willows*. This list is purposefully broad in time period, and many of the authors covered are not Catholic, again purposefully so. Children and young adults don't need to be given books that always align perfectly with a Catholic worldview; life will not afford them such a luxury.

Therefore, they need to be given tools to develop their faith and analyze it through the analogies of lived experiences that literature provides. All of the books used for discussion purposes bring up points of Catholicism and life that young people will likely ask about as they age; all of the books listed as suggested reading are ones that I have found helpful when reading with my children and when teaching and discussing with college students matters of Catholic faith inquiry. They are also all books taught now in private, public, and homeschool settings alike, and would make excellent additions to any family reading rituals.

I conclude this introduction with an anecdote. When my son was born eight years ago, one of my closest friends, a lifelong bachelor, sent him a letter. In it, he wrote that he was jealous that my son was just now being born. "You will get to experience all this world has to offer for the first time," he wrote. This line stuck with me as I thought about all my son would soon get to experience. My son's eyes at eight months old were bright, but when they looked around the room there always seemed a sense of surprise. I remember him best in a blue-striped swaddle blanket, where he spent most of his time, and me, then, trying to do everything that the new parenting books suggested I do, including walking him around my closet to see and feel the new colors and textures there.

My son always touched every fabric and seemed in awe of the colors and the feeling of the clothes; he'd often laugh when he'd feel or see something new, like a sequin or a feather, in the closet. Soon, the letter from my friend suggested, my child would know the pleasure of tasting ice cream for the first time and the joy of feeding ducks at the pond. He'd know the frustration of being unable to tie his shoes and trying over and over again—until one moment, understanding would finally click. He'd know the experience of feeling the wind in his face and hair as he would kick his legs higher and higher on the swing at our local playground.

My friend didn't write this in the letter, but I know, that one day, when he's older, my son will likely experience the thrill, pain, and joy of romantic love, too, and friendships that don't quite go as he expected. Promises fulfilled and pledges broken. He'll also experience grief. Like most children who grew up during the years of the COVID-19 pandemic, my recently turned eight-year-old boy has already encountered some of the hard edges of this world—has shared, and felt, suffering. Childhood has an inborn feeling of mystery, of things yet to come—both good and bad. All of it is new, enchanting. What is there be to be felt? What is there to be experienced?

When we read with children, we pause at the precipice of all this newness, or perhaps, more precisely stated, we decide to pause somewhere in the middle of some of these new, wondrous, good, and bad experiences. When reading, we reflect on our lives together, our children's lives, our own lives, where we are right then; we reflect with the children we read to, the children we hold close to us in a paused, stilled meditative moment. We might claim that reading is about acquiring and then mastering vocabulary—and it is in a utilitarian sense—but often this claim supersedes the love that overtakes our human community when we read together. Reading with children should not be transactional; it should be transformational.

Placing our Catholic faith at the forefront of reading with children centers, and makes present, this transformational claim. After all, we get to experience anew how children see the world, and we get the pleasure of talking with them about it. Moreover, when reading a book we've already read with a child, we get to experience rereading with new eyes and new hearts something we once loved, or perhaps didn't love, and to experience it all again alongside a new soul God entrusted us to share life with, to

Introduction

share his love with. When reading with children, we, in a sense, get to re*live* our childhoods. We get to re*live*, to re*know*, to re*experience,* and to re*fall in love with* our faith. As you start the first chapter of this book, I invite you to ruminate on this quote from another famous reader, St. Padre Pio. "In prayer and meditation," he says, "it is ourselves who speak to the Lord, while in holy reading it is God who speaks to us. Before beginning to read, raise your mind to the Lord and implore Him to guide your mind Himself, to speak to your heart and move your will."[28] May our hearts and our wills—and the hearts and wills of the children we love—be moved by the Lord as we seek to foster lives of holy reading.

---

28. Quoted in Bertanzetti, *Listening to God with Padre Pio*, 29.

1

Liturgical Living in *The Giving Tree* and *Cecilia's Magical Mission*

WHEN I CONVERTED TO Catholicism, keeping track of the liturgical calendar was an afterthought to say the least. This seemed to be a practice reserved for priests and others in religious life but not one that affected me necessarily. I'd notice changes in the color of vestments during Mass and vaguely appreciated the way the Church calendar affected my spiritual life on Sundays—yet it wasn't until the COVID-19 pandemic that I began to reflect on how I and my family marked our time. Working at home with two young children, with no noticeable change in days or activities, helped me to reevaluate this relationship. I realized that in my roles as full-time mom and teacher the school calendar dictated most of my life. From beginning each new academic year in the fall to picking up and dropping off my children each day based on their school bells, I discovered that it was the school calendar that signaled time change in our household. Christmas always seemed rushed. Advent was barely noticeable in my end-of-semester grading frenzy and the kids' activities, like pageants and parties. Ordinary Time seemed, well, ordinary.

Children's Literature and Liturgical Living

The pandemic helped me to realize that God wasn't at the center of my family's life because we weren't being obedient to his timing; instead, we were being controlled by our own human schedules—and usually those schedules were created by others' outside of our home. Strangely enough, it was a classic picture book, *The Giving Tree*, by Shel Silverstein, that helped to lead me to this conclusion. My daughter, then in kindergarten, found the book and brought it to me one day to read to her. I found myself unexpectedly crying as we read it aloud together, and I couldn't pinpoint exactly what had come over me. I remembered reading the book as a child, but I didn't recall this level of emotion attached to it. I was a little embarrassed, and I pondered over the next few days why I had reacted in this strange way. No doubt in part because of my unexpected reaction, my children wanted me to read the book again and again. As you might guess, again and again while reading the book together, I cried.

I even Googled whether I was alone in this reaction and soon discovered that the book inspired this emotion in others too—others who also weren't quite sure why they were crying. For instance, actress Chrissy Teigen tweeted out in 2016: "[C]an't read the giving tree without crying, despite having read it 100 times? What is the moral here?"[1] "What's the moral?" she asks, the same question I was pondering each time as I cried, reading the book with my children. This question it triggers is one the book naturally asks of us. Yet, importantly, it is one that most children's books ask of us, and it is the same question we find at the heart of our Catholic faith. How do we act morally?

While I don't know what Chrissy Teigen came to believe the moral of *The Giving Tree* was, for me—and for my children—we came to see it as a call to contemplate the changing seasons of our lives and how we treat others throughout those seasons. This led us to explore how to live liturgically as a family, or how to put the Catholic faith and its timekeeping and rituals (such as Mass, feast days, and sacramental rites of initiation) at the forefront of our lives.

---

1. Teigen, @chrissyteigen.

Liturgical Living: Finding Rhythms During the Pandemic, and Beyond

As I mentioned, the pandemic's sense of timelessness—of waking up each day in our house to perform the same activities day in and day out without much demarcation of time—led to my family reassessing our relationship with time. Even during months when COVID-19 didn't allow our local parish to offer in-person Masses, my family yearned for liturgy. The *Catechism* describes liturgy as "an action of the *whole Christ*."[2] This includes all within the Church—its priests and laypeople—those in the choir, servers, readers, commentators, and participants.

When we are at Mass together, we celebrate, through our actions, the wholeness of being in communion with Christ. When we could not be at Mass, my family felt a searing loss, and I was taken aback at how empty my soul felt. While Mass is the primary way the faithful celebrate together liturgically, the calendar of the Catholic church provides another rhythm of the year that binds its people. We have saints' feast days, special events in the life of Jesus, Marian apparitions, and important sacramental markers like First Communion and Confirmation that bind our actions as Catholics. While we could not attend Mass in person during the pandemic, my family began to feel solace that we could participate in liturgical life in other ways that would connect us to others. Once we finally were able to attend Mass again, we'd already discovered a new way of feeding our souls and celebrating our community within God's liturgical timing, reading the literature we loved with contemplative attention and a purpose aimed toward the divine.

The *Catechism* links words and actions together in its discussion of the significance of liturgy. It states: "A sacramental celebration is a meeting of God's children with their Father, in Christ and the Holy Spirit; this meeting takes the form of a dialogue, through actions and words."[3] During Mass, we not only offer signs of peace to each other via handshakes and prayer: We dialogue with God. Part of celebrating Mass is being open to God's presence through the words we offer in it, usually via scriptural reading and ritualistic prayer. Mass invites us to inhabit a sense of wonder throughout. In this context, wonder goes beyond curiosity and extends to marveling at God's mystery and our ability to communicate with him.

---

2. *Catechism of the Catholic Church*, no. 1136.
3. *Catechism of the Catholic Church*, no. 1153.

Liturgical Living

Often, during Mass, I'll find my children looking around the chapel, taking in the statues of St. Francis of Assisi and the Virgin of Guadalupe or staring at the stars in the center of our parish's colorful stained-glass windows. Mass is not the appropriate time to discuss the wonder children feel in those moments: It is a time for them to *feel*. However, we should encourage later discussions with our children about their feelings rather than forgetting these moments until the right time happens to come along on its own, which it rarely does in my experience.

Similarly, through reading, we create opportunities for imaginative exploration based on the sense of wonder children naturally possess. Thus, we can create similar sensory experiences as occur in Mass when we read children's literature together, reminding them of their previous feelings, tying those feelings to the readings as we delve deeper into what the feelings mean. We can then use these moments as launching pads to explore the awe that God embeds in their souls. Reading children's literature can become part of liturgical living because it encourages reflective experiences with words similar to what happens during the liturgy of the Mass itself.

The *Catechism*'s description of the sacramental celebration as a dialogue through words and actions mirrors my family's experiences of reading. It's a practice that, when enacted purposefully, reinforces how one experiences the wonder and spiritual engagement felt during weekly liturgy. Plus, reading together and then contemplating the meaning of the words encountered encourages parents and children alike to continue the practice of taking words and inscribing their meanings into their daily lives, as we do during and after Mass.

During Mass, homilies serve as a bridge between the sacred Scriptures and the lived experiences of the parishioners, offering interpretations for that day's scriptural readings. Theological frameworks used during homilies often apply two distinct, yet harmonious approaches to interpreting Scripture, approaches that can equally apply to children's literature—the moral and anagogical senses of reading. In the context of the liturgy, the moral sense of reading involves extracting ethical lessons from the scriptural passages used during the liturgy, guiding the faithful to align their lives with these teachings. The anagogical sense invites parishioners to consider the spiritual dimensions of the readings, fostering a deeper connection between the sacred texts and God's divine plan.

The Liturgy of the Word during Mass incorporates scriptural readings followed by a homily—an interpretation of those readings. Thus, Catholics are encouraged to engage spiritually with the transcendent dimensions of faith through contemplating words. The exploration of children's literature provides an opportunity to delve into a deeper understanding of various aspects of our Catholic beliefs, then, especially if we employ a comparable pattern of reading and the interpretation that we find in Mass. By reflecting on and discussing the literature we read together as families, we can attempt to discern the sacred in the ordinary and perceive deeper spiritual truths via religious symbols or messages woven into the narratives.

Living liturgically ideally extends beyond the confines of the Mass into our daily lives, molding not just how we interpret Scripture but also revolutionizing the way we approach the children's literature we encounter in our family cultures. Reading with moral and anagogical lenses specifically, unraveling ethical lessons and exploring spiritual dimensions, propels us beyond the literal or historical aspects of the words on the page. We practice these approaches throughout the year during Mass, and we can apply them in our domestic churches at home. These applications don't just reveal wonder; they potentially electrify our reading experience, injecting it with a deeper understanding of our faith and its compelling significance in our lives.

Exploring *The Giving Tree* by Shel Silverstein (Ages Four–Eight)

This brings me back to Shel Silverstein's classic 1964 book *The Giving Tree*.[4] I mentioned at the start of this chapter that this picture book helped my family to reconsider our relationship with time. Even though it is not necessarily a religious book, *The Giving Tree* brought us closer to the Catholic faith. The story revolves around the relationship between a boy and a selfless apple tree. As the boy grows older, he visits the tree, which gives him various parts of herself—her leaves, her branches, her apples, and her trunk—symbolizing acts of generosity. The boy uses the leaves to create a crown and play king of the forest; he swings from the branches and eats the apples. When the boy is a young man, he laments that he doesn't have any money, and the tree gives him apples to sell. When he grows a bit older, the tree provides him her branches and her trunk so he can make a house and a boat with them. When the boy comes back to her as an old man, the tree

---

4. Silverstein, *Giving Tree*. Because this picture book is unpaginated, page numbers are not provided.

is now nothing but a stump. The boy, now weary from age, seeks a place to rest and sits on the stump. At each stage in the boy's life, the tree is said to feel happy, particularly when he comes back from his adventures beyond the tree to visit her again.

I mentioned that when I read this book with my children, I cried—but my children did not. "That boy is not nice to the tree," my then–five-year-old daughter said when we first read it together. "He should have been nicer." When I asked her why she felt the boy wasn't nice, she said he used the tree, taking what he could from her but never giving back the love she showed to him. In this way, my daughter was using her moral imagination, though she would not have called it that. She was finding the moral of the story, relating it to her life, and determining how she and others should treat those they encounter.

My son, fifteen months her elder, helped to lead our family to an anagogical, or spiritual, reading of the picture book, though again he would not have called it that. "The boy should have played with the tree. He shouldn't have sold her apples or made a house from her," he said. It was he who inspired our family to understand that this book, for us, was about how we marked time. The boy in the story stopped giving emotional and spiritual time to the tree. "I am too busy to climb trees," the boy tells the tree as soon as he becomes an adult. This reported busyness is what hit home for us. The tree, more than anything, wants the boy to pause and spend time with her. He cannot imagine doing so, though. He does not cherish the ephemeral, spiritual moments of happiness he once had with the tree or the wonder they used to share when he was a child. He uses her for material gain, not spiritual or emotional growth.

When he is an older man who looks to be of retirement age, "the boy"—who is generally referred to in the story as such no matter his chronological age, just as we are referred to as God's children no matter ours—tells the tree, "I am too old and sad to play. . . . I want a boat that will take me far from here." The tree of course gives him her trunk for the boat so that he can "be happy," but now, he has, in turn, made her sad. "The tree was happy . . . but not really," Silverstein writes as we see the tree reduced to a stump. The picture shows the boy taking away the tree's trunk, the two hearts he had once carved on the tree to symbolize their love now separated. Based on the interactions he previously had with the tree, we readers can imagine that the boat does not make the now man in the story happy either. What would have made him happy was cultivating wonder and play with the tree even as he grew older. After all, he is happy as a boy when he loses himself in play with the tree, not thinking about what he can gain from her but rather how he can enjoy their time together. Their initial time together is about communion: It is about a loving, reciprocal relationship. He is shown smiling and jumping. There is awe and joy in his facial expressions and throughout his body when he spends time with the tree.

He becomes jaded as he grows up, though, seeing the tree only as a means to an end. His life is scheduled this way, too. He no longer marks time by how God would want him to or by what he loves; he begins to let his life be dictated by others' expectations. Every time he visits the tree, he says he is too busy to spend time with her. Every time she sees him, she says an iteration of the same thing: "Come, boy, come, play, and be happy." The boy, however, has lost his awe, his reverence for her. He never plays with her again, and he is never happy again. How many times as everyday Catholics do we say things like, "I don't have time for Mass this week. My work schedule is too busy"? Or, "I'm too tired to pray the rosary tonight"? How often are our schedules dictated not by God, or what would feed our souls, but by what the outside world recognizes as important? How often are we driven by busyness?

The moral within *The Giving Tree* reminds me of a passage from the Gospel of Matthew. In chapter 16, verse 26, Jesus states: "For what will it profit a man if he gains the whole world and forfeits his soul? Or what shall a man give in return for his soul?" The boy in Shel Silverstein's story, like the person mentioned in the Gospel, appears to gain materially from the tree but loses the deeper, soulful connection that once brought genuine happiness to the tree and the boy alike. The tree's constant invocation, "Come, boy, come, play, and be happy," echoes the divine call to prioritize spiritual fulfillment and meaningful connections over the transient gains of the world. There *is* time to play with the tree at every juncture of the boy's life. There *is* time for Mass and for praying the rosary. The boy simply stops recognizing worship and communion as a possibility for his life. Like my family was doing before the pandemic, the boy was letting the world, not love or God, dictate his schedule.

At the end of the story, the boy is too old to do anything but rest, and it is only then that he and the tree once again discover a semblance of happiness—together—yet it is just that, a semblance, and it is still incomplete. The boy can no longer play. He enjoys the tree's company only when he is too physically tired and frail to do anything else, and this is after he's used the tree over and over for material gain. "I don't need very much now," he says at the end of the book, "just a quiet place to sit and rest." While this communion may be enough to sustain the boy and tree in that sad moment as he sits on her stump, readers cannot help but remember all the times of rest the boy has missed out on earlier, times when he could have done more than rest from physical exhaustion.

He could have rested with the tree because he appreciated her company. Readers see—and, more to the point, *feel*—that the boy never has regrets or apologizes for the way he has treated the tree. It seems as if he does not recognize any of his faults, or sins. That is, the prescribed, timed world is so busy that it rushes this character from boyhood to elderly man with little room in between for contemplation of his soul or how he has treated the world and others. As he is on the brink of death as an elderly man, the man/boy does not seem to realize what he has missed out on in his short life. But, we realize, as contemplative readers, that what he has missed out on is everything that matters.

The pandemic forced the world to pause, as the tree invited the boy to do. This isn't to say the pause was for a good reason: Illness never is. Yet the pausing helped my family to reevaluate our lives before we got to the point that the boy did at the end of the story. As I read *The Giving Tree* with my two children and listened to their reactions, I asked them specifically about the boy's relationship with time. How was he giving his time? Both of my children said the boy should have played with the tree more and not given all of his time to work and material consumption.

The beauty of the liturgical seasons is that they inspire awe and provide opportunities for reflection that are distinct to their Church periods, much like the pauses the tree invited the boy to enjoy but that he missed in his rushed journey through life. The liturgical seasons, with their unique rhythms, call believers to embrace moments of reflection, gratitude, and connection with the divine, if they only choose to recognize them. This epiphany is what inspired my family to renew our celebrations of liturgical life. The story serves ultimately as a cautionary tale, urging us to break free from the relentless pursuit of worldly gains and instead to savor the timeless moments of wonder, communion, and liturgical living.

As Ecclesiastes 3:1–8 reminds us, "To everything there is a season, a time for every purpose under heaven." Every life, and every liturgical year, unfolds in seasons, each with its own purpose and meaning. We ought not let those seasons pass us by without contemplation or reverence.

Wondrous Reading

Exploring *Cecilia's Magical Mission* by Viola Canales (Ages Ten–Fifteen)

Soon after we finished *The Giving Tree*, a friend sent me a more recent book called *Cecilia's Magical Mission* (2019),[5] which also helped me to contemplate liturgical living in a new way. This book isn't a classic, but I believe it should be on all Catholic parents' bookshelves, especially as their children go through Confirmation—or if they simply want to contemplate the sacraments they've already gone through in a new way. My son went through Communion last year, and he isn't quite Cecilia's age in the book: She's fourteen. I plan to gift this book to him and to my daughter the moment they reach Confirmation age. I have already gifted it to their godmother, as the book focuses on this role in a serious way that I haven't encountered in most young adult fiction.

Cecilia's Magical Mission is essentially a coming-of-age story about a girl who is part of a Mexican-American Catholic community in California. In that community, everyone possesses a don, or a special celestial gift or talent that they discover as they move toward Confirmation. For instance, Cecilia's father helps people find lost things, or even parts of themselves. As such, his Confirmation saint was St. Anthony, whom you likely already know as the patron saint of lost things. Cecilia, however, struggles to identify her celestial gift, a concern that heightens as her Confirmation approaches.

What I love about this book is that it takes young people's faith struggles seriously, while advocating for a Catholic vision that is particular to Cecilia's cultural heritage while also true to the Catholic faith writ large. It is not often there are books that take faith seriously from a Catholic perspective. As Cecilia struggles with considering her future and her current identity, she is guided by her godmother, Carmen. Cecilia's mother loses a baby at the beginning of the story, and the entire community chips in to help with the funeral. Carmen helps to guide Cecilia's spiritual feelings about the loss of her sister. She tells one of Cecilia's friends, Julie, "As Cecilia's godmother it's my duty to have a '*plática*,' a talk with her about what just happened.... The plática will be about [her deceased] sister's soul." As many of us might be when we talk to young people about spiritual matters, Carmen worries Cecilia isn't listening to her—and certainly the younger girl struggles with paying attention during these times. Cecilia, for instance, is constantly

---

5. Canales, *Cecilia's Magical Mission*, 32.

Liturgical Living

worried about an upcoming school project, and she's also concerned that Julie, who isn't Catholic, will find the spiritual discussions that are common to her family strange.

Cecilia is listening in this instance with Carmen, though, and I'm going to provide the full discussion that comes next, so you can get a sense of how this book teaches about liturgical life. Carmen, sensing Cecilia has many questions about her sister's soul (as well as her own), tells her,

> Now, before you bombard me, let me begin by saying that the day of your baptism, the day I became your *madrina*, was about planting the seed of the Holy Spirit in your soul. Later, the talks we had when you prepared for your first Communion made that seed sprout. And now that your Confirmation is just around the corner the seed is to bear the fruit of your soul, when you take the next step and allow your *don* to manifest. Why? To help others: your family, your community, as well as yourself.[6]

Cecilia's magical mission is to go through Confirmation and discover what gifts she has that she can take to her community. Her godmother guides her as she discovers what she might have to offer those around her who most need it. At points, it's hard for Cecilia to see beyond the everyday world. She does not come from a well-to-do family. As she struggles with her faith, she tells her friends,

> Look, let me tell you both something: I know, or at least I have seen, all the people here, and they really are the same people who leave our apartment building every morning to go work as cooks, maids, and janitors. Many work two or three jobs coming home late at night. What kinds of *dons* are those? Huh? They're not wizards, for sure! Those are not gifts I want![7]

Cecilia, here, is confusing monetary rewards with spiritual ones, a theme we also saw in *The Giving Tree*. It's hard for her to respect spiritually those she sees as not having much money. She says here that she would prefer money to whatever spiritual gifts her community members have. Yet, her friends ask her to remain open-minded, which she ultimately does as she explores the unique gifts she can bring to the Church and her community.

One case for why Cecilia ought to broaden her thinking comes from the example of Cecilia's mother, Nica. The gift Nica discovers during her

---

6. Canales, *Cecilia's Magical Mission*, 32.
7. Canales, *Cecilia's Magical Mission*, 100.

Confirmation journey is cooking. She now owns a taco truck that serves the local community. We see Nica visit the community in her truck; she knows every person she serves food to, and she serves not only food but also spiritual and emotional guidance as needed. During her Confirmation, Nica chose the patron saint of Saint Nicolas, who allows "adults to be transported back to their childhoods."[8] Her gift, then, extends well beyond the cooking itself and into the myriad ways the cooking helps others and comforts them. Thus, it is not worldly riches that Confirmation is said to bring: It is spiritual ones. And these are what the book upholds as worthy.

Cecilia ultimately becomes an apprentice to Doña Faustina, whose gift is creating a coffee that helps people to contemplate their community gifts. Throughout her apprenticeship with Doña Faustina, Cecilia discovers that there is more to the spiritual world than she first thought: She and her friends, Julie and Lebna, even combine their school projects with Cecilia's journey to Confirmation. "Can spiritual gifts be proven?" becomes the basis for their joint science project, which they excel in by the novel's end, their teacher being interested in the topic and the girls' unique journey of discovery.

Eventually Cecilia embarks on a trip back to the Mexican village of Santa Cecilia, so she can help bury her baby sister there. This journey becomes a pivotal spiritual experience, where Cecilia discovers that her gift is similar to that of her mentor Doña Faustina. She creates a coffee ritual that helps soothe others' souls. The trip to Mexico teaches all the girls lessons about friendship, community, and the eternal struggle between the forces of good and evil as they face demons who want to stop their good work.

As most of you likely haven't read this book, it might sound like a contemporary fantasy novel, and it is perhaps for any readership who isn't Catholic. However, for those of us who believe in Confirmation and the power of the sacraments, it is a startling testament to what can happen if we live out our Catholic faith in its fullness—and relay its distinctiveness to our young people not merely on Sundays but throughout the wholeness of their lives. There could not be a better book about the power of liturgical life and taking the sacraments seriously. All Souls' Day features prominently, for instance, when Cecilia visits her hometown. Catholic rituals and calendars are the only timekeeping that seems to matter by the book's end. Cecilia's soul—and the spiritual mission she is on—is not the secondary aim, but the first aim of her life and the life of her community.

---

8. Canales, *Cecilia's Magical Mission*, 53.

Liturgical Living

When discussing the sacrament of Confirmation, the *Catechism* explains,

> The post-baptismal anointing with sacred chrism in Confirmation and ordination is the sign of consecration. By Confirmation Christians, that is, those who are anointed, share more completely in the mission of Jesus Christ and the fulness of the Holy Spirit with which he is filled, so that their lives may give off "the aroma of Christ."[9]

When people are confirmed, they take on new identities. Like Cecilia, they go on individual missions that are unique to their own talents and gifts. They discover their call, or vocation, and they learn that this calling is not about them, but about the betterment of the community in which they find themselves. They become part of the "fullness" of Christ's mission.

The final chapters of *Cecilia's Magical Mission* take place appropriately during the time of Advent. The three girls return to California from Mexico. During Advent, they feel "attacked and challenged and overwhelmed with even more mysteries."[10] As they prepare themselves for Confirmation, the book uses the liturgical season of Advent carefully. As you may know, the word "Advent" comes from the Latin word "*adventus*," which means "coming" or "arrival." Advent typically begins on the Sunday closest to November 30 (the feast day of St. Andrew) and lasts for four weeks, leading up to Christmas. In the Catholic Church, Advent is a time of spiritual reflection, anticipation, and preparation for the celebration of the Nativity of Jesus. It serves as a period of expectation and hope, not only for the commemoration of the historical event of Jesus's birth but also for his promised second coming. The liturgical color associated with Advent in the Catholic Church is purple or violet, symbolizing penance, preparation, and royalty.

Cecilia and her three friends await not only Cecilia's Confirmation but also the promise of the incarnation, or the Christ Child's physical birth in the world that Christmastide celebrates. The last page takes place on the Feast of Epiphany. If you recall, this book was published in 2019. Yet it suggests at the end that the girls, like the rest of the Catholic Church, will soon be fighting a particular evil in the world—perhaps "a worldwide plague that will kill many, many people."[11] Reading those words for the first time in 2021, I felt this book had unexpectedly portended a future where the

---

9. *Catechism of the Catholic Church*, no. 1294.
10. Canales, *Cecilia's Magical Mission*, 329.
11. Canales, *Cecilia's Magical Mission*, 330.

entire worldwide community would have to come together. Cecilia tells her friends after her Confirmation, "We've got a magical—life and death—mission to accomplish," as do we all who are Confirmed, as do we all who are guiding those will be.[12]

Living Liturgically through Reading

Pandemic-induced timelessness prompted a liturgical reevaluation for my entire family. Unable to attend Mass, our yearning for liturgy, and time marked by God's calendar, grew. Our return to Mass became a spiritual feast in and of itself that we will always remember. Celebrating communion with Christ and our community, we realized, was essential for our souls' nourishment. While waiting for this celebratory return, we found solace in imaginative reading, discovering connections, and reading in the interpretive ways we would Scripture. Although children's books are not divinely inspired, they are morally charged. We even found that we could make textual comparisons daily to the Church's Lectionary, the readings and responsorial Psalms ascribed to Mass each year and that are a part of the previously discussed Liturgy of the Word. In other words, we explored children's books with spiritual attunement, cultivating our moral imaginations in line with the Church's teachings and calendar and considering how the books might help to reveal God's truth.

In reading *The Giving Tree* together, my family found that the boy in the story positioned the world's calendar above God's, forfeiting his soul to fulfill his materialistic longings. That story was one of the first we read during that period that urged my family to reclaim wonder, live liturgically, and prioritize spiritual fulfillment over worldly desires. Returning to Ecclesiastes 3:1–8's wisdom, all of life's seasons impart a unique purpose. Even the difficult season of the pandemic helped us to discover truth and appreciate God's timing. It brought us to a fresh understanding of how literature can inform our faith paths, an idea that has sustained our souls and brought us closer together.

Enter *Cecilia's Magical Mission*, a contemporary exploration of liturgical living that emphasizes what's at stake in personal missional calls. Intertwined with her Mexican-American Catholic heritage, Cecilia's Confirmation journey illustrates the transformative power of sacraments. Like *The Giving Tree*, this novel emphasizes that the rite of Confirmation

12. Canales, *Cecilia's Magical Mission*, 331.

shouldn't focus on attaining worldly riches but on discerning spiritual gifts to serve the community. It should focus on God's love. The *Catechism* puts it this way, "Like Baptism which it completes, Confirmation is given only once, for it too imprints on the soul an indelible spiritual mark, the 'character,' which is the sign that Jesus Christ has marked a Christian with the seal of his Spirit by clothing him with power from on high so that he may be his witness."[13]

The "indelible spiritual mark" the *Catechism* speaks of signifies an enduring, unerasable imprint on the soul, symbolizing that the individual has been permanently sealed by the Spirit of Jesus Christ. In essence, this means that the person undergoes a profound, lasting transformation through Confirmation. This concept is vividly portrayed in *Cecilia's Magical Mission*. Here, Cecilia's Confirmation journey is not merely depicted as a one-time ritual but as a testimony to the enduring power of the sacrament. Much like the indelible mark mentioned in the *Catechism*, Cecilia's spiritual odyssey becomes a testament to the enduring significance of Confirmation, underlining her role as a witness to God's love and a bearer of spiritual gifts within her community.

To deepen reflection and spark a spiritual transformation like Cecilia's, and my family's for that matter, you might consider reading specific books during different periods within the Church's calendar as one way to lean into liturgical life. Create a ritualistic reading habit within your family that follows along with the Church's year. You might plan to read certain books at certain times within the liturgical calendar because of the topics they cover, or you might revisit certain books each year at the same time, deepening your reflection with the books themselves and with that particular calendar period.

Every year, my family, as many others do, reads the Nativity story together on Christmas Eve. As an augment to this practice, during Advent, we also read Barbara Robinson's *The Best Worst Christmas Pageant Ever* (ages eight–twelve). This annual reading tradition centered on a children's book adds a delightful and unexpectedly meaningful layer to our liturgical observance. The humorous and grace-filled classic has become a cherished companion to our Advent season. Our family inevitably compares our moral lives to those of the Herdmans, the Christmas pageant's unexpected stars. The book always sparks new spiritual conversations, and our collective hearts are filled afresh in time with the season. From a moral

---

13. *Catechism of the Catholic Church*, no. 1304.

interpretive frame, we usually recall that the joy the Christ Child's presence brings often unfolds in unexpected places. From an anagogical one, we usually recall that even amidst chaos and imperfection, divine grace has the power to shine through and transform lives, lives that are broken and sinful like ours often are.

Questions and Activity Ideas About *The Giving Tree* and *Cecilia's Magical Mission*

Included below are questions to prompt meaningful discussions with your children. Each question is paired with an activity, providing parents, catechists, and educators with creative opportunities to strengthen the children's connection with the book's messages. *The Giving Tree* activities delve into gratitude, generosity, and the joy of giving, while *Cecilia's Magical Mission* activities prompt reflections on faith journeys, the interplay of spiritual and material wealth, and connections to liturgical seasons. The goal is to turn passive reading into an active, engaging experience. Find more book recommendations and related questions on liturgical living in the appendix.

The Giving Tree: Questions and Activity Ideas

1. How does the tree show her generosity? How can we thank God for the beautiful nature around us, like trees? How can we show gratitude for the gifts we receive from God's creation?
   - **Activity:** Take a nature walk with your child(ren) and collect small leaves or twigs. Create a simple "Thank You, God" craft with these natural materials.
2. Can we find joy in giving and making someone else happy? How do we feel when we share toys or snacks with others?
   - **Activity:** Encourage your child(ren) to share a favorite toy or treat with a sibling or friend. Discuss the joy of giving and helping others.
3. What does it mean when the tree gives her branches and trunk for the boy's happiness? How could the boy have shown love back? How can we show love and sacrifice for our family and friends?

Liturgical Living

- **Activity:** Make a tree out of construction paper. On each leaf, write a way you can show love to family and friends.

4. How does the tree's love for the boy last throughout his life? Can we talk about God's enduring love for us, no matter what?

    - **Activity:** Listen to a children's hymn or song, perhaps one related to Noah and the ark, such as "The Wise Man Built His House Upon the Rock." Share your thoughts on how the song reflects God's enduring, sacrificial love. Draw parallels to the tree's love for the boy in the story.

Cecilia's Magical Mission: Questions and Activity Ideas

1. How does Cecilia's struggle to identify her gift mirror the challenges and uncertainties you might or have faced in your faith journey, especially when approaching sacraments like Confirmation?

    - **Activity:** Encourage readers to reflect on their own spiritual journeys. Ask them to write a letter to their future selves discussing the uncertainties they may currently face and their hopes for their faith journeys.

2. How does the book address the differences between spiritual and material wealth? How could you navigate similar concerns like this in your own life?

    - **Activity:** Organize a discussion or debate session where young readers can explore the values and priorities depicted in the book. Encourage them to share personal experiences or perspectives on spiritual and material wealth.

3. How are the liturgical seasons of Advent and Christmas used to enhance the narrative in Cecilia's Confirmation journey? What connections can be made between the characters' experiences and the themes of Advent and Christmas in the Catholic Church?

    - **Activity:** Create a collage representing the themes of Advent and Christmas as portrayed in the book. Discuss the symbolism and connections between the narrative and these liturgical seasons.

4. How does the mention of the Feast of Epiphany (January 6) and the hint at a future challenge tie into the broader Catholic understanding of liturgical time? How does it tie into the ongoing personal mission of those of us who have or who are about to receive the sacrament of Confirmation?

    - **Activity:** Facilitate a group reflection on personal missions and callings. Encourage readers to visualize their continued journey after Confirmation and establish individual spiritual objectives. On the Feast of Epiphany, gather for a special dinner where everyone shares their goals for spiritual growth. Capture these aspirations by writing them on slips of paper and placing them in a communal box. You might include notes like "I want to grow in patience, like St. Monica," or "Help me to serve others with joy, like St. Nicholas," or even small symbolic objects—handcrafted or chosen—such as a mustard seed for faith or a heart-shaped stone for love. Revisit and add to this box on each subsequent Feast of Epiphany, creating a tangible representation of the ongoing and evolving spiritual journeys within the group.

2

The Interplay of Faith and Reason in *Goodnight Moon* and the Magic Tree House Series

When my daughter climbed into the car after her elementary school art club the other day, she showed me a picture of a smiling green dinosaur on a yellow piece of construction paper. "Dinosaurs aren't real, right?" she asked me, looking from her creation to me expectantly. Her brother, a year older and therefore infinitely wiser than she—at least in his own head—answered for me. "Of course they're real!" he exclaimed, defending the honor of the creatures who had been his favorite subject matter from toddlerhood forward. I wasn't surprised my daughter expressed confusion about whether dinosaurs actually existed, though. In that moment for her, and for many of us often, it is a stretch to think that there was a time sixty-five million years ago when dinosaurs roamed the Earth.

When my son told her dinosaurs were real, she immediately ceased wondering otherwise, though. She quickly named her dinosaur "Carl" and pieced together quickly that he and those like him had been alive once upon a time. As readers likely know from their own experiences, children possess an uncanny ability to express wonder and awe. While that leap of acceptance from "Is something real?" to "It definitely is real" may have taken some time for many of us to arrive at, it took no time at all for my eight-year-old. As you may remember from the religious education you've experienced in years past, wonder and awe are collectively described as one of the seven gifts of the Holy Spirit. Following Isaiah 11:2–3, the Roman Catholic tradition asserts that a person receives these gifts during Baptism and that they are strengthened during Confirmation. Catholicism teaches that Jesus embodies all of these gifts perfectly, and they are also equally present in all Christians who abide in a state of grace.

Here, I ask readers to pause and to take in this last sentence once more. When we reflect on Jesus the human, we often reflect on his miracles, his strength, and his wisdom, but rarely do we think of the wonder he showed the world and the people around him. To be childlike does not seem as if it is the quality of a savior, perhaps. Yet we must remember that Jesus was not only a child of Mary and Joseph but also of the almighty God. When we think of Jesus, we ought to think of the baby at Christmas and the child in the temple as much as we do the adult preacher and divine king. In Matthew, chapter 8, for instance, we encounter the story of a Roman centurion, or officer, seeking Jesus's help to heal his paralyzed servant. The centurion explains that Jesus does not need to come to his house to heal his suffering servant: He knows Jesus can perform this act no matter where he is. Jesus marvels—or wonders—at the centurion's faith, relating to the crowd around him, "Truly I tell you, I have not found anyone in Israel with such great faith" (Matt 8:10).

Similarly, in Matthew 15, we encounter a Canaanite woman who, like the centurion, approaches Jesus with awe, or an unquestioning reverence for his capabilities as savior and healer. The woman seeks help for her demon-possessed daughter, shouting and begging for assistance when Jesus appears in front of her—not worrying what anyone might think. Jesus's disciples try to send this woman away, in part it seems because she is so passionate and sure of her mission. She is loud, but they ignore her. Likewise, Jesus initially states that he might not help her because she is a gentile. Because she is not Jewish, she is not one of "the lost sheep" of Israel. Her persistence and faith win the day, though. In Matthew 15:28, Jesus responds to her with wonder, paralleling his previous reaction to the Roman centurion. "Woman, you have great faith!" he tells her. "Your request is granted." Jesus commends the woman for her childlike belief, her wonder.

The belief this woman exhibited must have been extraordinarily difficult for her to maintain in the face of others who no doubt questioned *why* she would hold out such hope for her ill daughter, who seemed a lost cause, and *why* she would approach Jesus, who had a different genealogy

The Interplay of Faith and Reason

and religious tradition than her own. Significantly, we can perceive a repeated scriptural pattern of Jesus commending those who keep their faith in the face of every reason to believe they should not—and then expressing wonder that they do. The scriptural message is clear: We ought to have faith even in the face of adversity. We ought to imagine the possible even where others see the impossible.

Of course, the faith described above isn't that simple, no matter how nice that last sentence might look hung on a poster in an elementary school classroom or parish hall. As a convert who took years to come to Catholicism myself, I understand the dismissiveness of both the woman's friends and Jesus's disciples. What was the point of addressing Jesus when she was Canaanite rather than a Jew like Jesus? Moreover, why should the woman believe that Jesus could heal her daughter? I remember feeling quite alone when I began visiting Catholic Mass, fearing I did not belong in that beautiful, ritualistic space. Really, what was the point of my being there, when I came from such a different background and upbringing? I didn't know the words to the repeated prayers and was lost during the well-rehearsed, meditative movements of the parishioners. I often asked myself, "Why try something so foreign to what I was comfortable with and had known previously?" My friends and family asked many versions of this question of me.

Like every conversion story, the woman, like me, had to piece together what she knew of Jesus's past résumé with her burgeoning faith journey: She had to see the world differently from those around her, to try something new even when she likely felt lost and alone in doing so. What we find in most conversion stories like those of the Canaanite woman (and my own) is a *merging* of faith and reason. Too often in our cultural moment, we hesitate to combine these modes of inquiry, leaning on one more than another. The Canaanite woman relied on reason because she had heard of Jesus's miraculous healings in the past; reason germinated faith in her, faith so strong that Jesus himself expressed wonder at it. This combination of ideals is what Jesus saw in her and praised: He saw a logical belief in his ministry, founded on his past miracles, coupled with an openness to imagining a new world in which he could help her despite her different background. That latter imaginative leap is a perfect illustration of childlike wonder.

When I ultimately decided to convert to Catholicism—and then answered questions about my conversion from friends and family—it was not faith or reason alone that guided me, but the interplay of both in my head and heart. I spiritually felt God's call, but it was only after years of study and contemplation that the two fit together, and I decided to begin my official journey to enter the Catholic Church.

With this said, I wish now that it wouldn't have taken me the many years it did of attending Mass and reflecting on the faith before converting, and here is where I return to that story of my daughter at the beginning of this chapter. Children's innate ability to be amazed by the world around them is seen in Catholicism as a reflection of the openness and receptivity that we all ought to emulate as humans. It is a *reasonable amazement* that Jesus calls us to aspire to, a *reasonable faith*. Yet too often we bifurcate our lives. Faith is for church. Reason is for school. Faith is for the weekends. Reason is for the weekdays. Children ask "why" about it all, education and religion, and they do so fiercely and abundantly. Why is the sky blue? Why do we pray? Why do cows moo? Why does God love us? Too often, we, as adults, separate our answers to these questions into distinct categories; the Church does not.

Pope Francis, addressing the relationship between faith and science, aptly put it this way: "When we read about Creation in Genesis, we run the risk of imagining God was a magician, with a magic wand able to do everything. But that is not so." He emphasizes that God "created human beings and let them develop according to the internal laws that he gave to each one so they would reach their fulfillment."[1] This Church teaching reveals the compatibility of faith and reason, articulating a scientific understanding of Earth history and human development—yes, including the existence of dinosaurs—with the Catholic faith. When we talk about dinosaurs, we ought to talk first about God creating them and then what we know about them scientifically. The two ideas about dinosaurs are not separate in a Catholic understanding of the world. As Pope Francis reminds us, Catholicism invites us to appreciate the unfolding of God's creation through natural processes and the mysteries that tie faith and reason together into human understanding.

At this point in the chapter, you may have developed a certain "why" question yourself: Why does the compatibility of faith and reason matter when reading and contemplating children's spiritual engagement and literature? Here's one answer: In a study about the reasons children are disaffiliating, or leaving the Church, a full *one-third* indicated the perceived conflict between the Church's teachings and scientific beliefs played either

---

1. Schultz, "Pope Would Like You to Accept."

The Interplay of Faith and Reason

a somewhat or a very significant role in their decision.[2] Our culture may focus its talking points on other, more politically divisive issues that drive young people from religion, but a large swath of youth from elementary school forward are citing the conflict between faith and reason as a factor affecting their religious affiliation. Whether or not we mean it to, a bifurcation of belief systems and a perceived disconnect in the conversations we have about faith and reason is hurting our children's spiritual lives. Katherine Buliniski, an associate professor of geosciences at a Catholic university in Kentucky, Bellarmine, relays,

> Every semester I encounter students who are absolutely amazed to learn that faith and science are compatible within Catholicism, some of whom had the benefit of more than twelve years of prior Catholic education, and they are left wondering what to do with this new information. Unfortunately, I think that by this point in a young person's life reconnection with the Church may be a difficult path and the revelation of the compatibility of faith and science is not an especially compelling reason to reconnect.[3]

We cannot put the onus on children to make connections between seemingly disparate disciplinary subject matters like religion and science when the prevailing culture and media tell them the two do not fluidly connect. If religious and scientific education never intersect in our conversations with the children we care for, why would these children think to connect them on their own? How would they know how to do so? This slippage between faith and reason in our teaching and cultural discourse often leads to disillusionment in the Church and later to disaffiliation.

Most scholarly literature and writing about how to merge faith and reason come from Catholic scientists and teachers like Bulinski. Usually, they discuss two ways of understanding the world that they impart to pupils, which ultimately helps their learners connect the dots. We ought to begin teaching children these two ways at far earlier stages of their lives than when they enter or go through college. A theological or philosophical understanding derives from personal faith and divine revelation. It emphasizes spirituality, sentimentality, and morality. A scientific understanding of the world derives from empirical observation and experimentation. It emphasizes objectivity, repeatability, and variability. Stated simply, one way of knowing gets at why the world works the way it does and the other at

---

2. McCarty and Vitek, *Going, Going, Gone*, 5.
3. Bulinski, "Science, Truth, and Disaffiliation."

how the world works that way. I contend that literature, *especially children's literature*, uniquely melds these two ways of knowing and ought to be used as a tool to aid the development of both, guiding children to best discover the fullness of the truth.

Literature is neither solely theological nor solely scientific. Yes, it teaches young audiences how to understand the world and often imparts reasoned knowledge, but we approach it differently than we do a science or history textbook. Consider historical fiction like Patricia McLachlan's *Sarah, Plain and Tall* or Mildred D. Taylor's *Roll of Thunder, Hear My Cry*. In these books, children learn historical and scientific facts about late-nineteenth-century farm life in the US Midwest and the tumultuous background of the civil rights movement in 1930s Mississippi. They do so via stories that inspire their imaginations rather than limit them through rote memorization. Literature invites a sense of wonder and active engagement with whatever subject matter it examines. Through reading stories, children and the adults who care about them can engage in meaningful conversations about how faith and reason work together to create a fuller understanding of subjects like science, math, history, philosophy, and art. They can connect the dots of their other studies, with wonder at the forefront.

In his "On Three Ways for Writing for Children," Chronicles of Narnia author C. S. Lewis shares, "The modern view seems to me to involve a false conception of growth. They accuse us of arrested development because we have not lost a taste we had in childhood. But surely arrested development consists not in refusing to lose old things but in failing to add new things?"[4] More and more, children are leaving religion behind at the same time they are leaving reading storybooks with loved ones behind, and this is happening at younger and younger ages. A 2023 national reading survey from Scholastic reveals that children are now stopping reading for fun by age nine, a dip from 40 percent to 28 percent.[5] A major factor is that grown-ups no longer read with children; they expect them to read independently. Children also add extracurricular activities, which detract from family reading time.

As C. S. Lewis points out, we seem to assume that part of growing up means abandoning "old things," and part of what our society is abandoning as children mature into adults is reading together, as well as alone. Devaluing reading, and the creative and analytical skills it offers, devalues religion

4. Lewis, "On Three Ways of Writing for Children," 46.
5. Clark et al., "Reading Trends."

as a natural byproduct. When imagination is set aside, so is a propensity for wonder and awe at God's creation.

Literature sparks imagination with new knowledge, and we ought to encourage our youth not only to combine those two ways of understanding the world from their very youngest days, but also not to leave reading behind as they grow older. We ought to keep encouraging reading, even as we add more social events to our children's calendars. We ought to maintain a supportive reading culture in our roles as families and educators, discussing ideas within books together, and engaging our imaginations collectively within our respective communities, even as our children learn to read on their own. That is, we ought not give up one good because we have found others. We can harness the power of literature to explore the conversations that children may not be having when they move from one subject to another in their educational pursuits—as they move from their weekday thinking to weekend thinking.

The two books this chapter explores are Margaret Wise Brown's 1947 classic picture book *Goodnight Moon* (ages zero–six) and Mary Pope Osborne's wildly popular contemporary Magic Tree House series (ages seven–twelve). I've chosen these books because most children today are likely to encounter them at home and in school. Caregivers can begin cultivating children's and young adults' sensibilities to contemplate faith and reason together from the youngest of ages using literature's special ability to combine wonder with academic growth. Furthermore, both books are typical of their respective genres.

Examining how parents and educators can use them as springboards for discussion will naturally aid adults when they seek to foster a harmonious integration of faith and reason in the young minds they nurture as they read other, similar books, too. In sum, by delving into the beloved pages of *Goodnight Moon* and the thrilling adventures of the children in the Magic Tree House series, adults can initiate conversations that extend beyond regurgitating plot, actively shaping a child's formative years with a focus on spiritual attunement and emotional growth.

Exploring *Goodnight Moon* by Margaret Wise Brown (Ages zero–six)

Goodnight Moon is probably one of the most well-known children's classics ever composed. A favorite gift of friends to mothers-to-be at baby showers and grandmothers to grandchildren, it has sold more than forty-eight million copies.[6] It consistently tops children's literature bestseller lists still, and its widespread popularity spans the globe, with translations of it appearing in at least a dozen languages, ranging from Spanish to Hmong—the language of an indigenous people in Southeast Asia. I remember my mother reading this book to me about twenty-five years ago on an old, tan, corduroy couch in our living room, the musty smell of our sofa cushions merging with her flowery favorite perfume that had mostly worn off during a long day at work.

I also remember reading this to my children while they were in the womb, believing the lulling language would bring their kicking feet some peace. Expectantly, I waited for the day I could read it to them after they were born. Most recently, I remember my daughter reading the book aloud to me, exuberant she could take the reins at story time. The words "And a comb and a brush and a bowl full of mush"[7] rolled off her tongue delightedly as her fingers simultaneously rolled over Clement Hurd's illustrations of each object. Likely, you too have some memory of *Goodnight Moon* in your childhood or adulthood, either reading it or having it read to you.

Although we are used to our twenty-first-century picture books being grounded in reality, when Margaret Wise Brown composed her little masterpiece, it was widely hailed as the first of its kind. Prior to 1947, most popular children's picture books were fairy stories or fables, taking place in faraway lands with princesses, ogres, happily-ever-afters, and pat moral lessons. Brown believed children would connect more deeply with stories rooted in their daily experiences than those that were fantastical. She embraced and popularized what has been dubbed the "here-and-now" storytelling philosophy. This approach emphasized that young children, in their exploration of the world, could be captivated by narratives centered on straightforward, everyday activities—such as the ritual of saying goodnight before bedtime. Brown wanted to meet children where they were, detailing the world around them, the world they knew, rather than delving into a fantasy world entirely different from their everyday existences.

The plot of *Goodnight Moon* is simple. The story recounts a rabbit saying goodnight to everything in his vicinity, both animate and inanimate. It includes a series of goodnight wishes to familiar and seemingly random things, such as the room, the moon, a red balloon, a young mouse, and

---

6. Crawford, "Surprising Ingenuity Behind *Goodnight Moon*."
7. Brown, *Goodnight Moon*, n.p.

The Interplay of Faith and Reason

more. The repetitive structure and soothing language create a calming and familiar atmosphere, rendering it a treasured, almost hallowed, bedtime story. As the rabbit gradually says goodnight to each item, the illustrations depict the transition from a brightly lit room to a darker, nighttime setting. The narrative and illustrations work together to create a peaceful and reassuring bedtime ritual for young readers and their caretakers, culminating in the rabbit saying goodnight to the entire world. "Goodnight stars. Goodnight air. Goodnight noises everywhere," reads the last, famous, poetical lines. Even when simply writing these words, my nervous system calms, and I breathe in a little deeper, appreciating the imagined stars and the textured silence.

This book guides even the youngest children in naming and honing what they know. Bedtime rituals are almost always a part of children's daily lives, a pattern they can point to as part of the logic of their, and others', lives. From brushing their teeth to saying their prayers, almost all children have a routine they follow. Beyond this realistic plot, Brown depicts objects most children are familiar with as well: The setting is "a great green room" that contains, among other items, "a telephone" and "a little toyhouse," staples of almost all households and childhood experiences. Even if children do not possess these objects in their own homes, they are probably aware of others who do.

This simple book guides young children to use reason, then. After all, children are probably used to experiencing an evening like the one the little bunny does in the book when he prepares for bed. Plus, children are probably used to the types of objects he focuses on, regular household items they can look around their own rooms and spot. In *Goodnight Moon*, children who are as young as toddlers use the patterns they recognize in their own life and reason out how a similar ritual with similar objects appear in a bunny protagonist's life. There are no surprises in this book, only logic and a focus on the material world—well, almost no surprises.

This "almost" part is where I believe wonder occurs. *Goodnight Moon*'s magic lies in the bunny's appreciation for each material and immaterial object he comes across. He acknowledges them all by saying goodnight to them, appreciating how they make his life better. Wonder in Catholicism is seen as a gateway to recognizing the divine presence, and this recognition naturally gives rise to gratitude. In the spirit of nurturing wonder and awe in the hearts of little ones, the biblical verse Psalm 19:1 comes to mind: "The heavens declare the glory of God; the skies proclaim the work of his hands." Just as the young rabbit bids goodnight to the objects around him, expressing wonder at their existence, this verse reminds us that the objects and the places they reside are "the work of his hands." Identifying, marveling, and appreciating are all steps ordered toward worship. I believe this book's spiritual pattern is what makes it feel calming to the soul. Illustrator Clement Hurd's son, Thacher, suggests that the book "mirrors what's happening for [child readers], but it also gives them a feeling of some other world, something else that's sort of a larger, more peaceful world."[8]

This world, I propose, is the spiritual one, and the feeling of comfort children and adults feel from Brown's language and Hurd's illustrations are a result of our human connection to the spiritual world. This book never claims in any way that it is religious in nature. Indeed, its "here and now" storytelling seems to claim the opposite. Yet the lulling power of "a larger, more peaceful world" that lurks beneath the material one we fondly remember appearing in the book, like that "bowl full of mush," is what I believe enchants audiences and keeps them coming back to the book's beloved pages.

Even the order of the book's illustrations and identification of objects bespeaks the natural order of the world and how humans imaginatively relate to it. Take a moment and remember your childhood room, or where your bed or mat lay as a child if you did not have your own room. My room was quite small. When I would sit there and play with dolls during the day or listen to music on the radio at night, I now realize I felt the room contained the entirety of existence. Even thinking back now, knowing the room was tiny, it still looms gigantically in my mind. This is where I lived, where I dreamed, played, thought, prayed, and even held court with neighborhood friends while we made friendship bracelets or pretended we were royalty while sipping our afternoon tea.

It is where I chatted on the phone for hours about goings-on at school and where I cried into my pillow on various days when I had dessert taken away, and, on a specific day, when I found out my grandmother had died, had been taken away, too. While to most outsiders, the room might have seemed small, to me it was indeed a "great green room" (and ironically it *was* actually green). My room was the centerpiece of my life. I cannot begin to tell you how many times I studied objects in it as I sat up in bed at night—the alarm clock and the lamp on the nightstand next to me, breathing them in almost to the point that they were part of my body and soul.

---

8. Blair, "*Goodnight Moon* Has Comforted Kids at Bedtime for 75 Years."

The Interplay of Faith and Reason

I knew, and still easily recall, every wood scratch on the lamp's base and precisely where I had to turn the dial on the radio to get the best reception for the local AM gospel station, the only one my parents said I could listen to at night.

In Brown's book, the rabbit, just as I did throughout my childhood, sits in his bed and gazes upon his room's expanse, feeling it is huge. He first stares at small, physical objects like the telephone next to him. Then he begins gazing at the pictures on the wall—the art chosen and hung for him by someone who cares about his comfort. These grab his full attention. Readers are provided two full-page illustrations devoted to the room's paintings, the "cow jumping over the moon" and "three little bears sitting on chairs." Again, similarly, I remember staring at a picture of a rainbow over a little house nonstop before I went to bed at night. I ask you to consider again for a moment: What art did you have placed in your room as a child, and what art have you hung, or would you like to hang, in a nursery or school? How did the art you looked at as a child affect you emotionally, and what factors might go into a decision to hang a piece of art in a child's space today?

In considering these questions, you'll likely arrive at the opinion that we hang art for children in large part because we want them to be inspired by beauty and joy. We want to instigate their smiles when looking at the art. We want to pique their imaginations. Like humans generally, the rabbit is attracted to the paintings' aesthetic, creative expressions, moreso than he is the book's other listed objects, such as the telephone, that do not merit the same full-page illustrations or his attention. While I do remember the scratches in that lamp's base next to my bed, I instinctively smile at the memory of the brightly colored rainbow that graced my bedroom wall. Objects evoke memory; paintings evoke emotion.

Significantly, when we take time to contemplate art as the rabbit in the story does, we are prompted to consider the divine source of creativity. When reading picture books with children, we are provided with an opportunity to discuss with child readers why art fascinates us. Through art's beauty and emotional resonance, we glimpse the mysterious and transcendent nature of God. We imagine why artists painted what they did, and we merge our imaginations with their renderings. In imagining why that cow jumped over the moon, for instance, we participate in creating the art because of our responses to it.

As a parallel, our engagement in God's creation involves not only our responses to it but also our connection with him. Painter Mark Rothko articulates the reciprocal and interactive essence of art, where both creator and audience play a role, stating, "A picture lives by companionship, expanding and quickening in the eyes of the sensitive observer."[9] Appreciating art is an act of co-creation; our reactions are intrinsic to its aesthetic impact. Art's beauty lies in its ability to mirror human responses, even in its static state. For instance, the Mona Lisa's smile may appear judgmental or welcoming, depending on the observer's state of mind. Rothko underscores his belief that art evolves and improves through the sensitivity of viewers. Similarly, as integral components of God's creation, our responses to the world can contribute to its betterment, mirroring how our appreciation enhances art. We possess the capacity to enrich the world by responding to God's continuous invitation to worship, a beckoning that perseveres regardless of our circumstances or perspectives.

Although this book is geared primarily toward helping adults guide children through reading literature together, it would be remiss of me not to point out that in "reading" books like *Goodnight Moon* with children who cannot easily read words yet, it is they who have much to teach their adult companions. Once we learn how to read, we often skim over the pictures on a page. However, for child readers, it is the opposite: They spend time staring at the pictures and interpreting the stories therein first and foremost. Pictures in picture books aid not only children's burgeoning abilities to read words but also their abilities to create and interpret stories. Reading picture books combines faith (trusting one can put together a narrative story without knowing what the words are) with reason (learning language).

Unlike children, adults are used to focusing on what they know, the words on the page. As such, they will often miss artistic details and connections. To use Rothko's verbiage again, child readers are naturally more "sensitive" when reading picture books, an idea that perhaps extends to the world at large, considering how children interact with spaces other than books, spaces filled with words that might change by their image-oriented perceptions.

My seven-year-old is a struggling reader, but she points out the smallest details in picture books that I often miss, such as how an image in a story adds a layer of meaning to it. She helps me to notice that the colors in *Goodnight Moon* gradually dim like the close of day. Child readers are used to interpreting the world through aestheticism and their reactions and observations have much to teach the adults who might be long trained in

---

9. Kalabekova, "Viewing of the Painting as Deep Emotional Experience."

The Interplay of Faith and Reason

thinking in a linear, language-focused way only. Childlike wonder encouraged to develop through picture book art can, in and of itself, help adults stir a part of their spiritual selfhoods that may have atrophied over time. The bunny in *Goodnight Moon* communicates the essence of children's experiences as they navigate their lives by interpreting the world—God's creation—primarily through their senses rather than relying on language. Reading this book with the children we love can remind us that the world is not only understood through words but also through another vibrant language of colors, shapes, and emotions.

In *Goodnight Moon*, after gazing at the art in his room, the rabbit then lists other objects like a "comb" and a "bowl full of mush," veering his attention away from something that requires more of him, like art, to other things that do not. Once our emotions are settled through a focus on the objects, he brings himself and his readers back to something of consequence in the room, "a quiet old lady . . . whispering hush." While we do not know with certainty who this woman is in relation to him, we can assume she is someone who cares about the bunny—his mother, grandmother, or nanny perhaps—and who is lovingly coaxing him to sleep. Like the paintings, the "old lady" receives a full-page illustration. We see her knitting as she sways in a rocking chair and minds the rabbit. This moment is another emotional escalation in the book; we journey from objects, to art, to objects, and now to a beloved one. We travel back and forth from the material to the immaterial, a cornerstone of Catholic teaching. As the Nicene Creed reminds when we attend Mass, "the Father almighty" is "maker of heaven and earth, of all things visible and invisible."

To accentuate this point, the next page of Hurd's illustration zooms out and we see the entire room displayed on two pages, with one illustration taking up both: The rabbit locks loving eyes with the woman nurturing him from across the room. Hurd's artistic mastery captures the magic of the moment—a room bathed in the warm glow of love. In this shift to a panoramic view that encompasses both the rabbit and the woman who tenderly watches over him, we transcend the rabbit's singular viewpoint, assuming an omniscient stance that allows us to witness the profound connection between both parties. As we gaze upon Hurd's illustration, we find ourselves not just observers but participants in this intimate scene—part of God's creation unfolding within the pages—privy to the material and the immaterial. The act of stepping back, relinquishing a narrow viewpoint, mirrors the rabbit's earlier contemplation of the art adorning his walls. It beckons us to ponder: Are we, too, "sensitive observers" of the beauty and love present in the world around us?

Next in the book's "plot," we repeat the series of goodnights to everything the rabbit has pointed out to us previously, the rabbit never rushing from thing to thing but fully appreciating and spending time in wonder on each object. At this point, we reach what I identify as the crescendo of the book. "Goodnight stars. Goodnight air" appear on the penultimate pages before the rabbit falls asleep. The rabbit in his own small way has come to be grateful for what cannot be described physically, "stars" and "air." We have reached a metaphysical moment in the book, another way of knowing beyond the material. The "stars" and the "air" appear on one, huge, illustrative connected page together, a series of clouds at the bottom of the page with stars interspersed at the top. We are no longer in the rabbit's room: We are outside of it, moved to something bigger—grander—than even this room is the rabbit's small, but gigantic to him, world.

When we are taught about God in our youth, we often imagine heaven as the sky and God's answers to our prayers in the air rustling around us. The famous gospel hymn "How Great Thou Art" is predicated on this oft-used metaphor of connecting wonder and awe with this type of imagery. The hymn begins:

> Oh Lord my God, when I in awesome wonder
> Consider all the worlds Thy hands have made
> I see the stars, I hear the rolling thunder
> Thy power throughout the universe displayed.

Those last lyrics—"Thy power throughout the universe displayed"—could be the title of Clement Hurd's illustration of the stars and air that the rabbit studies in his room. I believe the peacefulness we feel at the end of *Goodnight Moon* is because the rabbit intuitively feels at peace with the universe, with God.

The rabbit has thanked him for every object, for beloved objects and caregivers, and now he gives homage to the creator of it all. And he falls asleep peacefully, as have millions of readers wrapped in the warmth of this worshipful love. Although Brown never explicitly mentions God, readers sense his peace and love in the rabbit's explorations of his surroundings. If they paid attention to that philosophical or theological other way of knowing, God was guiding them all along. The ending is where faith and reason harmoniously converge—an unspoken acknowledgment of the divine embedded in the simplicity of a child's bedtime ritual. Reading this book resonates with our shared experiences as spiritual seekers, prompting us to revisit it repeatedly and pass down its comforting synergy to future generations.

Exploring the Magic Tree House Series by Mary Pope Osborne (Ages Seven–Twelve)

Readers of the Magic Tree House series will likely recognize a familiar trope. In the series, eight-year-old Jack and seven-year-old Annie stumble on a familiar portal that takes them to a fantastical world. When C. S. Lewis created The Chronicles of Narnia series—probably the most iconic work within the portal fantasy genre—he popularized a trope that automatically begs the question of how to merge faith and reason. The protagonists in each set of books discover a portal that transports them to extraordinary, magical realms. For Jack and Annie, the portal is a magical tree house filled with enchanted books; for the Pevensies, it's the wardrobe leading to the fantastical land of Narnia.

The ways in which C. S. Lewis inspired young readers to see the immaterial within the material, to look beyond the veil, so to speak, can be found in Osborne's work today. For those of you who haven't read or heard of the Magic Tree House series, it is today's most widely known and popularly used book series to teach children how to read. The first book in the series, *Dinosaurs Before Dark*, was published in the year 2000. Now, there are over fifty books within the series, and new books are continuously being added. To date, it has sold over 134 million books globally and been translated into at least thirty-five languages. A teachers club website for the books explains the series's unique, stepping-stone approach to reading:

> The Magic Tree House look now clearly delineates a reading journey through three distinct lines: Magic Tree House titles for beginning chapter book readers, Merlin Missions for more advanced readers, and Fact Trackers for nonfiction fans. By renumbering the 55 fiction titles in two groups (plus a Super Edition!), we are encouraging readers to stay with their favorite series longer, giving them a sense of accomplishment as they move from the classic adventures into the Merlin Missions.[10]

This book series is often among the first chapter books children read, replete with illustrations by Salvatore Murdoch and Natalia Boyce. Moreover,

---

10. Magic Tree House Teachers Club, "Celebrating 25 Years."

it is often one of the series children stay in longer than others because it aims to age up with them as the series progresses. I have yet to meet a child recently who has not at least heard of this series, and most I know have read something in it. Like *Goodnight Moon*, it is likely the children you are reading this book for and/or will have encountered these titles. Thus, they are a perfect platform for discussion.

With this said, these books are not written by C. S. Lewis: They do not have an overtly Christian perspective, nor is that their aim. When Jack and Annie climb up the wooden ladder into the portal, they embark on adventures of reason. They find information, facts. Yet, just as all good fiction does, the facts merge with imagination and take the children to new historical worlds. They have to discern what is real and what is not real in these worlds, and I believe the books do a vast service to parents who want to talk to their children about how not only to merge faith and reason but also to discern what is true and what is untrue. When do you know when you're encountering a fact in this book, and when do you know when you're in the realm of the imagination? Perhaps no better series offers parents and educators the chance to discover their children's responses to our modern world and to help guide those responses.

One of the reasons my children love the Magic Tree House series is that Jack and Annie are different from each other. For the purposes of this discussion, I'm going to use examples from the first book in the series, but you will be able to transfer the interpretive ideas I offer to others in it. Throughout the series, Jack is the more rational child. He carries a journal with him, in which he records facts about the places and time periods they visit, acting as a scientist and ethnographer. Annie is different. She is intuitive and relies on her emotions to guide her. Jack and Annie embody the two different ways of knowing the world.

We see this first in how the children stumble on the tree house itself. Annie runs toward it. The afternoon is "lit with a golden, late-afternoon light," suggesting she is running toward somewhere ethereal.[11] Although he whispers, "Wow," as he stares at the grand tree, feeling awe, Jack cautions Annie not to climb it: "No! We don't know who it belongs to," he exclaims.[12] But up they go, and once he follows her up, Jack is overcome with seeing the books scattered around the tree house. The knowledge offered overwhelms him. While he tries not to touch the books, only surveying their covers,

---

11. Osborne, *Dinosaurs Before Dark*, 1.
12. Osborne, *Dinosaurs Before Dark*, 1.

The Interplay of Faith and Reason

Annie cries out that she has found one Jack will be interested in. "Here's a book for you," she says, holding "up a book about dinosaurs." Osborne writes that even as he protests, Jack opens "the dinosaur book to the place where the bookmark was. He couldn't help himself."[13]

Neither Jack nor Annie are perfect children in this scenario. Cautious parents like me might be alarmed they are taking such risks! Yet we see what tempts Jack and Annie, and these are opportunities to ask our children what might tempt them the most in Osborne's tree house. What knowledge would they most like to have access to? What historical periods would they like to visit if they had a tree house like Jack and Annie's? What knowledge would they most like to have? Annie flips through a book about castles, probably one similar to the kind my Disney-princess-loving daughter would gravitate to. Annie also understands what would interest Jack—the dinosaur book—and offers it to him, knowing the type of personality he is. She is attuned to emotions in a way Jack is not.

When they discover that Jack's wish to see the dinosaurs he is reading about has led them to the time period in which dinosaurs existed, both of them search for truth and understanding about how they came to this place and also about the creatures they are meeting. They spot a Pteranodon outside the tree house. Annie tries to talk to him. Jacks reads in his book about him:

> The flying reptile lived in the Cretaceous Period. It vanished 65 million years ago with the dinosaurs.[14]

Jack tells Annie it's impossible they are where they are, but she readily accepts it. Like my daughter when she asked about whether dinosaurs were real, Annie readily shows faith that the seemingly impossible can, and has, happened. Leaving the tree house, she

> touched the Pteranodon's crest. She stroked his neck. She was talking to him.
> *What in the world is she saying?* Jack wondered.
> He took a deep breath. Okay. He would go down, too. It would be good to examine a Pteranodon. He could take notes like a scientist.[15]

---

13. Osborne, *Dinosaurs Before Dark*, 7.
14. Osborne, *Dinosaurs Before Dark*, 13.
15. Osborne, *Dinosaurs Before Dark*, 16.

Annie tells Jack that the Pteranodon is "nice" and that he should touch him, instead of simply writing about him. "Don't think, Jack. Just do it," Annie encourages.[16] Jack is rewarded with a pleasant interaction. "Fuzzy skin," he writes in his journal, and readers are now rewarded with a picture of Annie caressing the dinosaur, her eyes big and wondrous, while Jack smiles at the two of them, writing his ideas about the experience with a large smile on his face.[17]

Again, while Jack, the rational thinker, approaches situations with caution and a scientific mindset, Annie embodies the intuitive and emotional side, readily embracing the seemingly impossible. In the context of faith and reason, these characters can be seen as allegorical representations of those two different ways individuals engage with the world and seek understanding. Jack's methodical approach, recording facts and observing the world, mirrors a scientific understanding of the world—relying on empirical evidence and logical reasoning. On the other hand, Annie's emotional and intuitive responses resonate with a more philosophical or theological perspective, where faith and trust play essential roles in understanding the mysteries of existence. It is only because these characters are together that we get the fullest sense of the situation. We know the facts from Jack; we know how the dinosaurs feel from Annie.

This moment is a happy one, but the climax of this book is not as easy. Annie trusts her instincts, telling Jack that a Triceratops they discover "looks nice."[18] She gives the dinosaur a flower, offers her beauty, which the dinosaur readily accepts. Though Jack had cautioned Annie not to approach this dinosaur, he begrudgingly writes "nice" in his journal. Then, Annie has an instinct that is anything but nice; she senses the Triceratops is feeling afraid. She looks around, her eyes resting on a Tyrannosaurus Rex. The Magic Tree House series may seem to center on gleaning facts, but Annie's intuition saves the children from harm time and time again. Additionally, Jack's opening himself up to Annie's way of viewing the world and Annie's opening herself up to his negotiate the scenes that matter and the children's emotional growth as humans. Again, like *Goodnight Moon*, spirituality is never mentioned specifically, yet we can make connections for our children that seem implicit in these narratives. Ideally, children will be able to spiritually read what is happening in the world—to engage in

---

16. Osborne, *Dinosaurs Before Dark*, 17.
17. Osborne, *Dinosaurs Before Dark*, 17.
18. Osborne, *Dinosaurs Before Dark*, 26.

The Interplay of Faith and Reason

these two disparate ways of knowing—without always having it spelled out for them in ways so didactic that the learning feels forced or ignoring it so that it feels as if only the scientific understanding makes sense.

The most memorable moment in this first book in the series, and the picture that splashes across the cover, is when cautious Jack leaps on the back of Pteranodon to escape the Tyrannosaurus Rex who is in pursuit of him. Jack is terrified, now facing a monster who stands between him and the tree house, which symbolizes safety. Jack first looks to his reference book about dinosaurs for answers. He reads,

> Tyrannosaurus Rex was one of the largest meat-eating land animals of all time. If it were alive today it could eat a human in one bite.[19]

The book is no help, he decides. The Pteranodon, whom Annie had befriended, swoops down. "Don't think!" Jack tells himself and leaps on its back, literally taking a leap of faith as Annie's earlier words about not thinking so much when he first meets the Pteranodon come rushing back to him.[20] Jack and the flying dinosaur share what is dubbed in the chapter title an "amazing ride."[21] The word *amazing*, according to the *Oxford English Dictionary*, dates back to the Middle Ages and means "[c]ausing great surprise or wonder; astonishing, astounding."[22] I link this here because we see Jack at the end of the Magic Tree House series experiencing *wonder*. He no longer records what is happening like a scientist, though that is still a part of him, but he adds faith to his knowledge, and this is what saves his life and ignites a grand adventure. What child, or what adult for that matter, would not want to take flight on the back of a befriended dinosaur? When Jack merges faith with reason, his personal story, and his soul we might read into it, literally take flight together.

In his encyclical *Fides et Ratio*, or Faith and Reason, St. John Paul II begins with these words: "Faith and reason are like two wings on which the human spirit rises to the contemplation of truth; and God has placed in the human heart a desire to know the truth—in a word, to know himself—so that, by knowing and loving God, men and women may also come to the fullness of truth about themselves."[23]

---

19. Osborne, *Dinosaurs Before Dark*, 47.
20. Osborne, *Dinosaurs Before Dark*, 52.
21. Osborne, *Dinosaurs Before Dark*, 52.
22. "Amazing," *Oxford English Dictionary*.
23. John Paul II, *Fides et Ratio*.

At its core, the Magic Tree House series is about the pursuit of truth. If as Catholics we believe the fullness of the truth emerges only when faith and reason work symbiotically, it is easy to read Jack's flight and his journey toward that dramatic plot point as a metaphor for what we and our children can aspire to if we merge these two ways of knowing. In realizing whether or not we tend to lean toward one way of understanding the world over another—in realizing our desires and how we are most apt to pursue truth—we can work to balance the scales so that we, like Jack and Annie, may attempt a more harmonious journey toward the fullness of truth. In this way, the Magic Tree House series can serve as a literary lens through which we can reflect on our own cognitive and spiritual landscapes, as well as those of our children, considering how faith and reason intertwine in our quest for understanding God's universe and our positions in it.

Integrating Faith and Reason through Reading

In the peaceful scenes of *Goodnight Moon* and the enchanted realms of the Magic Tree House, the unifying force of storytelling integrates faith and reason in a way similar to how our brains work. As we take in new knowledge, we must, as humans, integrate that knowledge with what we know already of the world. We cannot section off knowledge as if the world were divided into school subjects that never merge. Through reading, we can work to teach our children how to think in unifying ways, rejecting compartmentalized ways of knowing and opening up imaginative possibilities.

As Catholic readers, we are charged with the special task of exploring truth with an eye ever toward deepening spiritual understanding that reveals the great truth—God's plan for the world. In *The Confessions*, St. Augustine puts it this way: "Reason is the soul's gaze. But since it does not follow that everyone who gazes sees, a right perfect gaze, from which vision follows, is called virtue."[24] In other words, we, like the rabbit in *Goodnight Moon* and Jack and Annie in the Magic Tree House series, all have our own "gazes" of the world through which we understand—or reason out—how that world works. None of us boasts a single, perfect gaze of the world. In trying to calibrate our perceptions of it and our attendant limitations, we must, ultimately, depend on our virtue. That is, we ought to aspire to see the world not only reasonably but also well, to see beyond our own gazes to that of God's gaze.

24. Augustine, *Confessions*, 4.

Thus, we should be open to learning from others. When we read books about characters similar and different from us, our gazes broaden and deepen as we make comparisons from the characters to ourselves. Books open us up to wonder, and wonder opens us up to truth. In the Magic Tree House series, Jack and Annie develop in virtue because they value each other's way of thinking and intuiting. As readers—or to bring Rothke back in our conversation, as sensitive observers—of books that explore faith and reason, we can mimic the characters' virtues in combining faith and reason. We can make art through reading. Indeed, the more books we read, the more models for both good and bad ways of perceiving the world we have and the more virtuous we can become.

Like Jack and Annie, we must try to navigate the world by being open to holistic ways of understanding, always mindful of our own limitations. It is in this open-mindedness and self-awareness that we, too, might experience flights of amazement akin to Jack's, propelling us toward our most important ascent to God.

Questions and Activity Ideas about *Goodnight Moon* and the Magic Tree House Series

Included below are questions to prompt meaningful discussions with your children. Each question is paired with an activity, providing parents with creative opportunities to strengthen the family's connection with the book's messages. *Goodnight Moon* activities explore familiar objects, bedtime routines, and imaginative play, while the ones paired with the Magic Tree House series inspire reflections on teamwork, overcoming challenges, trust, and creativity. The goal is to turn passive reading into an active, engaging experience. Find more book recommendations and related questions on the interplay of faith and reason in the appendix.

Goodnight Moon: Questions, with Activity Ideas

1. Point to and name familiar objects in your room. Why do you need each object for bedtime?
    - **Activity:** Set up a sensory bin with objects related to bedtime in *Goodnight Moon* (e.g., a toy bunny, a comb, a brush). Allow

Wondrous Reading

children to explore the objects through touch and play, reinforcing their connection to the story.

2. What is your favorite part of saying goodnight, like the bunny in the story?

   - **Activity:** Have your child create a visual bedtime routine chart with images of their bedtime rituals. Next to it, create a chart of God's "bedtime rituals," such as the sun setting, the moon and the stars coming out. Hang the chart next to the child's bed.

3. If your toys could talk, what do you think they would say to you at bedtime?

   - **Activity:** Using construction paper or felt, craft simple puppets representing the characters in *Goodnight Moon*. Encourage the child to use these puppets for imaginative play, reenacting scenes from the book or creating their own bedtime stories about their toys and activities.

4. Can you point to the moon in the sky? What color do you think it is when you say goodnight to it?

   - **Activity:** Create a simple lullaby together, incorporating elements from *Goodnight Moon*. Sing about saying goodnight to different objects, the moon, and God, fostering an emotional musical connection to your child's bedtime routine.

Magic Tree House: Questions, with Activity Ideas

1. Jack and Annie work together to solve problems and go on adventures. How does teamwork help them in their quests? How can working with others help us to understand things better in real life?

   - **Activity:** Craft decision-making story cubes by drawing or printing images related to various choices. Roll the cubes and have the child(ren) create a short story based on the images. Draw or attach images representing various choices on each side of the cube. For example, you might have one side with a picture of a forest, another with a spaceship, and so on. Add small stickers or labels with numbers to each side for easy reference during the activity.

The Interplay of Faith and Reason

   Discuss how using both imagination and reasoning can lead to interesting and creative narratives.

2. Jack and Annie often face challenges on their adventures. How do you think faith can help us when we face difficult situations? How might reason help us? What are the advantages of combining the two?

   - **Activity:** Create a "faith and reason jar" with your child or children. Write down situations where they might need faith and reason (e.g., making a new friend, solving a problem at school) on slips of paper. Whenever they face a challenge, they can pick a slip and reflect on how both faith and reason can help them navigate it.

3. Jack and Annie often have to trust the magic tree house to take them to the right place and time. Can you think of a time when you had to trust in God and use reason, even if you didn't know exactly what would happen? How did it turn out?

   - **Activity:** Write down different scenarios where faith and reason play a role (e.g., starting at a new school, trying a new hobby, making an important decision) on cards. Have the children pick a card and act out the scene while others guess what is happening. After the guessing, discuss how both faith and reason can guide us in uncertain situations and help us make good decisions.

4. How do Jack and Annie use their imagination to solve problems in the Magic Tree House stories? How can our creativity and imagination, inspired by the Holy Spirit, help us to solve problems in our own lives? Can you think of an example when you've creatively solved a problem?

   - **Activity:** Have a storytelling relay. Start a story with a problem, like a dinosaur attack. Each person adds a sentence or two to continue the narrative, focusing on imaginative solutions. After the story is complete, discuss how the Holy Spirit can inspire our creativity and imagination to find solutions.

3

Culture of Life in *Alma and How She Got Her Name* and *Little Women*

There's a story I'm a little ashamed to tell, but I suspect it might resonate with some readers of this book, so here it is. A few days before our first child was born, my husband and I sat in a parking lot together and cried about how our growing family would change the one we already knew—the family we shared as a couple. It had been a night that felt perfect in every way: The food at the Italian restaurant was great, the weather was beautiful, and we had laughed all night with other couple friends with whom we simply clicked. As we sat in the parking lot before driving away, the stars shining above us, we discussed the life together that we feared we might soon be giving up: going out whenever we wanted, traveling on a whim, magical nights with no curfews—the life we knew, this life. Quite frankly, and embarrassingly, having our son felt like a threat to our romantic selves. We knew we shouldn't vocalize it or perhaps even feel this way, but we did. We cried. We mourned. We feared.

It bears mentioning that my husband and I had been trying to have children for almost six years by this point, and that we'd had trouble getting pregnant. Discovering I was going to have a child had been an ecstatic, joy-filled moment. We had cried happy tears when we'd discovered there was a baby on the way. Likewise, we had cried deluges of tears over the years, worried we might never welcome a child into the world. Thus, in no way was this parking lot moment indicative of my entire pregnancy. Yet it was a true moment, and I mention it at the start of this chapter centered on a culture of life because it's probably a more authentic, resonant moment for many now than it was in generations past. When we look back on this moment, as my husband and I sometimes do, we talk about how little we knew of the world then. In bolder, more honest moments we talk about how selfish our musings were then.

Although my husband and I had yearned for a child for years, we could never have prepared ourselves for the moment our newborn son opened his bright, curious eyes and looked into ours for the first time: It felt transcendent. The years afterward, with my son, and later with his sister, have often felt transcendent, too. I suspect other parents know this struck-by-lightning feeling, the feeling that you are no longer concerned solely for yourself, but suddenly just as much for this other little self in front of you. You are you, but you are also now you split in half.

The world is bigger, the love you feel for it deeper, grander. My spouse and I could never have explained to our past selves what the experience of having children would be like: the joy that more life in our midst would bring to us, to our understanding of the world, and to our relationship with God and each other. Rather than detracting from our senses of who we were personally and as a couple, our son transformed our senses into a different, better, and deeper relational framework of personhood, couplehood, and family.

Whether or not we realized it, my husband and I prior to our son being born had in some ways been conditioned through the media and other cultural touchstones to view new life, even life we had collectively prayed for for years, as somewhat of a threat. Though Catholic, we still faced social pressures from outside of our faith. We both worked in professions at the time in which we were often the lone Christian, much less the lone Catholic, voices in the room. We worried that having children would affect our economic situation and our career opportunities, in addition to our freedom as a couple.

Pope John Paul II, in his 1995 encyclical *Evangelium Vitae*, or "The Gospel of Life," recounts that our society has become increasingly obsessed with individualism, particularly exalting the "isolated individual in an absolute way."[1] Accordingly, the individual who is stronger and can exert his or her will over the weaker is the one who will end up with the most power

---

1. John Paul II, *Evangelium Vitae*. All references to this encyclical in this chapter come from this document.

and satisfaction in society. As a couple, my husband and I weighed our individual happiness—our romantic lives, our careers, and our economic situations—and placed those in competition with the demands a new child would bring to our lives. Yet that momentary weighing of values in the parking lot that night was not because we did not want a child: We did! It was because we were acutely aware of the consequences of having a child for a family, and we felt the social and economic pressure of our changing life situation.

Moves today toward solidarity and community, including the decision to have a family, are often undermined by a broader cultural shift idolizing individuality. This cultural emphasis leads to the fragmentation of social bonds and a weakening of communal structures that have traditionally provided support and a sense of belonging for families. Generation Z and Millennial parents like my husband and me therefore worry, probably more than young people did in generations past, about the disruption a potential child could bring to our lives, knowing we are risking some individual freedoms society holds dear. Further, unlike in generations past, there aren't as many structures in place in the form of tight-knit communities to support those who choose to have families, especially larger ones.

In his encyclical, John Paul II adds,

> If the promotion of the self is understood in terms of absolute autonomy, people inevitably reach the point of rejecting one another. Everyone else is considered an enemy from whom one has to defend oneself. Thus society becomes a mass of individuals placed side by side, but without any mutual bonds. Each one wishes to assert himself independently of the other and in fact intends to make his own interests prevail.

This perspective is a reminder of the consequences of a culture that prioritizes individualism over community. How often do we hear today that we have the answers inside ourselves? That all we need to do is look within and we will find all we need? If we do not need each other, and we only need ourselves, then we are side by side but without "mutual bonds," as Pope John Paul II states above. Inevitably, with this social ordering, we begin to view each other as competition rather than as social partners and aids.

Almost every Disney movie my daughter watches seems to impart this individualistic preference, as do most TikTok and Instagram social media influencers. I worry that such autonomous fetishization leads to a feeling that relying on others makes a person weak rather than offering strength. If we all wish to "assert" ourselves, then we, whether or not we explicitly say so, are pitting ourselves against each other instead of aiming to support each other. Disney's 2023 film *Wish*, which came out around Christmastide, featured a song with the following lyrics:

> If you're try'na figure out who you are
> You're a star!
> ...
> It's all quite revelatory
> We are our own origin story![2]

Asha, the main character, is told she need only look within to "figure out" who she is. There is no "origin story" she needs to hear beyond being her own star. Her individualism is the "revelatory" center of the world, just like everyone else's. Community, much less transcendence, is a fiction in a world in which everyone is a "star" and whatever is inside of one is all one needs to understand oneself.

Asha is not led to anything greater, as the wise men were when they followed, or we might say wished upon, a star and journeyed to Jesus, a journey demonstrating a quest toward reaching and understanding and a good far greater than the magi could find within themselves. Stated another way, the magi were not their own stars and could not offer their own revelations; they were following God's star and his divine revelation. Scripture reminds us that the magi look beyond themselves in their part of the Christmas story, as we should, in our stories seeking Christ here on Earth.

Matthew 2:1–2 reads, "After Jesus was born in Bethlehem in Judea, during the time of King Herod, Magi from the east came to Jerusalem and asked, 'Where is the one who has been born king of the Jews? We saw his star when it rose and have come to worship him.'" The wise men, the magi, traveled a significant distance, according to biblical scholars, a distance between eight and nine hundred miles, from Persia to Bethlehem. They did not make this dangerous, arduous trek to honor themselves but to *worship* the Lord, to welcome not only a human baby but also the son of God who would bring salvation to the world, salvation to others *beyond themselves*.

Significantly, the wise men's journey reflects the incarnational reality of Christianity—the belief that God became flesh and dwelt among us—that he sacrificed for our world because we as human individuals cannot save ourselves on our own. The incarnation denotes that life and

---

2. Michaels and Rice, "I'm a Star."

community are not found in isolation or self-assertion, but in relationship and in self-giving love. Just as the wise men sought out Jesus, and just as Jesus sacrificed himself and loved the world, we are called to seek out and support one another, recognizing that our true identity and fulfillment are found in communion with others and with God.

This incarnational and relational sense of self is set in stark contrast to the ubiquitous, self-centered messaging we find in today's individual and personality-obsessed media. Pope John Paul II's vision of a culture of life emphasizes the inherent dignity of every person, while focusing on the importance of recognizing that dignity through forging and maintaining relationships and solidarity. A culture of life recognizes that fulfillment is found not in isolated pursuits, but in connections with others, in the mutual support of family and community. We are not all isolated stars perfect in our own selves; rather, communally, we are seekers of the beauty we see beyond us in the stars that make up the wondrous cosmos that surrounds us—all of us.

Reflecting on the principles of a culture of life can help children, and the adults who love them, to unsettle the cultural norm that apotheosizes, or exalts, individuality at the cost of all other ideals. In his book *Becoming a Eucharistic People: The Hope and Promise of Parish Life*, Timothy P. O'Malley laments that no matter how often one speaks to others about the doctrines of the Catholic faith, or the beautiful gift of communion and the Lord's sacrifice in words and deeds for the world, explanations alone, no matter how smart or backed by however much evidence, are not what most humans are seeking. He writes, "The crisis in the Church and world right now is not only intellectual. It is a crisis of the heart, a forgetting of the desire for total communion that is the destiny of every man and woman."[3]

Through literature, we can reach children's hearts, to remind them why communion matters and how they can practice it and begin to attune their lives to it. Moreover, we can practice this togetherness with them. During Mass, we celebrate togetherness with our parish communities: We do so with each other and with God. By reading stories with our children, we can help to frame their consciousness outside their parish communities for those times when they are being led astray from "their destiny" as humans toward "total communion" with God. We can help them to discern when they are consuming stories about individual autonomy that are potentially detracting from the fullness of life they can have with God and with all

---

3. O'Malley, *Becoming Eucharistic People*, x.

those about whom they care and are placed in front of to serve. We can also help them to celebrate and revel in stories that convey the truth and goodness found within spiritual and emotional communion. Intentional reading, I dare say, can help children and adults alike to reach their shared destiny of total communion.

In her best-selling book *Reading Magic: Why Reading Aloud to Our Children Will Change their Lives Forever*, Mem Fox points out that reading as a practice in and of itself celebrates community and togetherness, especially if reading aloud is employed. When we read together, we initiate a ritual that bonds children with us. We snuggle. We hold each other. We commune. Even in group settings, we usually sit in a circle, or, at the very least, we sit silently, with reverence for the moment, enjoying each other's bodily and emotional presence. Plus, the stories we read with children during this time can foster a culture of life both in the experience of enjoying each other's presence and in the content we choose if we are thoughtful about what we are reading and how we are talking about the reading during and afterward.

Fox, an expert in literacy education and a popular children's book writer, imparts the following about reading books aloud with children:

> As we share the words and pictures, the ideas and viewpoints, the rhythms and rhymes, the pain and comfort, and the hopes and fears of big issues of life that we encounter together in the pages of a book, we connect through minds and hearts with our children and bond closely in a secret society with the books we have shared. The fire of literacy is created by the emotional sparks between a child, a book, and the person reading. It isn't achieved by the book alone, nor by the child alone, nor by the adult who's reading aloud—it's by the relationship winding between all three, bringing them together in easy harmony.[4]

Recall what theologian Timothy P. O'Malley said about the crisis within the church today being "a crisis of the heart." Reading aloud with children can help to mend this crisis, to eliminate the tendency to overexplain doctrine and to under-attend to matters of the heart. If we thoughtfully connect what we read together with the larger issues young people care about—and the issues we want them to care about—we can help to ignite that emotional spark through the bond that reading literature together naturally begets. The words on the page, the ideas, the closeness, the brain activity,

---

4. Fox, *Reading Magic*, 10.

the spiritual connection: All of it occurs in concert when reading, and all of it potentially contributes not only to fostering a culture of life but also to encouraging young people feel they want to participate, and already are participating, in a vibrant reading community with an adult lovingly guiding and reading with them.

This chapter focuses on two books, a contemporary and a classic one, both of which celebrate a culture of life in distinctive ways that provoke conversation and communion. The first is Juana Martinez-Neal's picturebook *Alma and How She Got Her Name* (ages three–nine), which is published in readable (and adorable) English and Spanish editions. It won the 2019 Caldecott award, the highest honor given to picture books for children in the United States. In this pre-K and early-elementary-school-age book, Alma Sofia Esperanza José Pura Candela feels she has too many names—six in total! Her father sits down with her and explains to her the history, and person, behind each of her names.

Together, Alma and her father read about and look at family photos. We see her sitting in his lap with a book, imagining her past and thinking about who she is. The book celebrates a culture of life as Alma wonders at how all of these family members have led to her and to her story today. Catholic readers will particularly appreciate an homage to some of the Candela family traditions that are worth pointing out and enjoying with young child readers—my children love pointing at pictures of Mary and comparing our sacred traditions, as well as discussing how Alma's family differs from ours.[5] This is an excellent book, one of my favorite recent Caldecott winners, and I cannot wait for you to read more about it.

The other book featured in this chapter is Louisa May Alcott's 1868 classic *Little Women*, another one dear to my heart and, I suspect, dear to many readers of this book as well. Importantly, this novel was made famous *not* because it was passed down through the public education system, like many other classics we commonly know today, but because generations of women readers read it aloud together in their domestic spaces and passed it down to each other from one generation to the next. That is, *Little Women* was shared through time, one lifetime to the next, usually from one mother

---

5. Although this chapter focuses on the many positive symbols and iconography in this book, I am not suggesting it is a perfectly Catholic text. Like many other texts we are encountering in this book, it is a popular one, and it is often used in public and private schools, not to mention its popularity on library shelves. Catholic audiences will notice a mix of religious and secular symbols, which should and can produce rich discussions.

to her daughter and so on and so on, from 1868, up to the present day. Talk about a culture of life through reading!

The first section, or book 1, of *Little Women* focuses on the four March sisters, Meg, Jo, Beth, and Amy, as they explore who they are individually and, importantly, who they are in community. The second section, book 2, focuses on the sisters' emergence from childhood into young adulthood, keeping to the themes of the individual in community. Alcott's novel is a time-tested exemplar that can be used to talk with children and youth about a culture of life. Plus, it is one in which we as adults, by reading it with those younger than ourselves, can continue a tradition that generations of readers have been a part of before us. Reading it, especially reading it aloud, is a nod to the past and a continuation of building up a culture of life through the generations that many Catholics might find appealing as a tradition to carry forward not only as a familial and educational bonding experience but also as a spiritual one.

Exploring *Alma and How She Got Her Name* by Juana Martinez-Neal (Ages Three–Nine)

When you look at the cover of *Alma and How She Got Her Name*, you see a round-faced, smiling, rosy-cheeked girl, with a pale pink bow in her pixie-cut black hair. Wispy bangs are off to the left side of her face. She looks to be about four or five years old. She's wearing pinkish-red striped pants and a white T-shirt with a pink heart on it, which is barely visible because her hands are clasped in front of her. She's holding a pencil with her right hand, and her index fingers are touching, a little like Michelangelo's creation of Adam fresco in the Sistine Chapel, where God touches Adam's hands, giving him life. The picture is a happy one. Alma's buoyant, round eyes are looking left and slightly up. Above her, in big block letters is printed her name, ALMA, and it and looks as if she's colored her name in that same pinkish-red as the stripe on her pants with the pencil she's holding. There is a bird above the M, and it seems that the bird, with a little pink wing and cartoonish face, is looking down on her.

"My name is too long, Daddy," Alma complains in the first few pages, "and it never fits." Alma is trying to write something, it seems, and having a hard time signing her six-word name on the page.[6] Readers don't

---

6. Martinez-Neal, *Alma and How She Got Her Name*. All quotes and references come from this version of the book. Picture books are unpaginated.

know what she's writing, but her dad pulls down a book from a shelf. She snuggles up with him in a chair, and he prepares to tell his daughter the story of her long name. Already, we see the two of them, cuddling and reading together, performing that reading magic that literacy educator Mem Fox refers to as transformative. The bird we see on the book's cover follows Alma on each page.

First, Alma's father tells her about Sofia: her grandmother, his mother. She loved "jasmine, flowers," and, "of course," her son, or "me," he says to his daughter, smiling. "She was the one who taught me how to read," Alma's dad tells her, as he teaches her to read. Sofia's picture, on the right side of the page, shows her with a book, and you can see the connection between the picture of Alma with her daddy and what it must have been like for him to be with his mom, learning to read, a generation before, probably engaging in a similar conversation and activity.

The next moment begins the book's refrain after Alma is introduced to a new family member and meaning for her name. Alma calls out delightedly that she appreciates her second name—Sofia: "I love books and flowers . . . and you, too, Daddy!" she declares. "I am Sofia!" she exclaims. Whereas on the previous page, Alma looked a little pensive, a bright smile now lights up her face. She touches a beautiful, pink blossoming tree, sits atop a stack of books, and looks radiant. Alma learns that she is an individual connected to a community of family members who love her. She is herself, but she is also a member of a family. She is Alma *and* she is Sofia—not simply in that she shares the name Sofia but also in that she shares part of Sofia's identity. Sofia's traits are transposed onto her own. She shares Sofia's love of particular material objects, such as the books and the flowers that her dad mentions. Plus, she shares the loving bonds with family, such as the kinship with her father, that Sofia felt. They both love him! Not only do they both love her father, but they also love reading with him. She and Sofia even look alike.

The clearest Catholic symbolism occurs a few pages later when we learn about Pura, another of Alma's name inspirations. Alma's father shares, "Pura was your great-aunt. She believed that the spirts of your ancestors are always with us, watching over us." The page on which we see Pura is awash with religious symbolism. Pura in Spanish means pure, also translated as immaculate. The image we see of Pura shows her lighting a candle, and Alma tries to do the same, standing behind her with her own, smaller candle: Alma's face is joyous, her eyes particularly so. Her smile is so big that she is squinting. Alma's father stands behind her and holds a candle that is already lit. He gazes at an Immaculate Heart of Mary on the wall that looks to be part of a sacred prayer space in the house. His expression is far more serious and contemplative than it has been during any other part of the book.

In the prayer space that expansively opens up on the right side of the page, readers see Alma and Pura surrounded by various religious and cultural symbols, including Indigenous folk art. A large Sacred Heart of Jesus hangs to the upper right above Alma's head, as do a few different artistic renderings of the Immaculate Heart of Mary. Directly above Alma stands a statue of Mary on the wall, fixed on a wooden pedestal. The statue is about as big as, if not bigger than, Alma. Mary holds her immaculate heart, offering it to the room and the world. Pura is situated in front of both Alma and Mary. She is dressed in a veil and long, flowing, robe-like dress: She resembles the Virgin Mary.

In fact, when we first read *Alma* together, my daughter, then in pre-K, pointed at the picture of Pura and identified her as the Virgin Mary without skipping a beat. Hence, I would suggest, the religious symbolism is clear to even the youngest of Catholic readers. At the time, my daughter could not read the words on the page at all, but she was able to interpret the iconography. Pura's face reveals a peaceful smile. When reading with children, adults can point to the compassionate love the Virgin Mary has for her family, including her son, and the love he offered the world. Pura's love, the love she shows through prayer, the hearts we see, and the candles being lit, are perfect moments to talk about the Catholic faith. Alma learns about God and her family's love as she learns about her name and her Great-Aunt Pura's faith life.

In particular, the picture featuring Pura presents an ideal moment to speak of the Immaculate Heart, the source of Our Lady's fiery and ever burning love for God, and Catholics' desire to try to imitate her love. The candles in the room, along with the fire we see wrapped around all the versions of the Immaculate Heart of Mary, remind Catholic audiences that their relationships to family are centered on God. It even makes sense that Pura's story is the center of this book: It is central to the story, the heart of Alma's journey and that of the readers. Luke 2:51 suggests devotion to the Immaculate Heart of Mary: Jesus's "mother [Mary] meanwhile kept all these things in memory, meaning in her heart." This verse displays Mary's contemplative, compassionate, and feminine role in the church, a role echoed by Pura, who draws the spiritual thread through Alma's story; she keeps the memories of everyone, including the religious history Alma needs.

We see the prayer space, gendered feminine with Pura and her devotion to the Immaculate Heart, occupied by Alma, too. Although Alma stands behind her great aunt, she is still covered by the same bluish-gray color scheme that is Our Lady's and that takes up most of Pura's page. It bears mention that Pura is kneeling as she lights a candle, and Alma is leaning forward, behind her, learning how to pray: Alma is not yet fully kneeling but is arched forward, leaning, learning. Alma's father, on the other hand, is squarely outside the space the two women occupy. He is standing upright on the far left of the page. He gazes upward and reverently at the bright blue Immaculate Heart, but, again, he is separated from Alma and Pura on the page's right side.

His devotion and religiosity are apparent, yet theirs is distinctive, feminine, and Mary-centered with its hues and iconography. Alma's back is halfway in the space with her father, but she is mostly in the room with Pura, leaning that way as mentioned, and she is bathed with the light of the prayer space. Like most children, Alma will have to decide if this Catholic-infused area is where she wants to stay. She looks happy there, but she is young, and there are other cultural pulls for her attention, as there are for children today.

When you turn the page, two special things happen that make this book an especially important one and an especially glorious read. First, the color scheme changes to a brighter blue. Alma still wears pink, and she stands close to Pura now, side by side, leaning into her, now with their eyes connecting. Pura looks more Marian than ever, wearing a simple blue robe and veil cascading to the ground. She still smiles, peacefully and grace-laden. Candles in jars hang above the two, and the imagery is reminiscent of Pentecost. As you likely recall, Pentecost is celebrated fifty days after Easter and commemorates the descent of the Holy Spirit upon the apostles and other followers of Jesus. It marks the beginning of the church's mission to spread the gospel. Alma's book, in a way, is a decision about whether she will continue her Catholic story and whether she will continue to spread the gospel.

Here is where I believe the book becomes most interesting! Atop one of those candles, on the left side of the page, with Pura and Alma on the right, sits that little bird that has been following Alma from the title page through every page in the book. On the page I just described, the one with the prayer space, the bird is perched atop Alma's head. This bird, I believe, can be interpreted as the Holy Spirit following Alma as she learns about her family, her spirituality, and where her story leads. The type of bird Alma has around her is never mentioned in the book, but the image could certainly be an illustration of a dove. Because the bird's type is never specified, it seems even more that it could very well be an artistic rendering of the Holy Spirit, who is not a character in this story but a guiding force in the little girl's growth.

The dove, as I'll call the bird going forward, is perched above Alma's head at the beginning and the end of the picture book, too, the only times it is seen in this position except when Alma is in the prayer space. Significantly, young readers follow pictures more than words. Importantly, this story is told in a picture book format, and in it, we see a dove following a little girl as she learns about the generations that preceded her and considers what her own story might be in light of those who came before her. She is guided by the Holy Spirit throughout, represented by little dove following her in every picture, as well as by a woman named Pura who is devoted to the Immaculate Heart of Mary. You might recall Alma's dad stating that Pura is a woman who speaks of "ancestors watching over us"; more traditional Catholic readers might prefer to call these human ancestors saints. These are the types of faith-filled conversations one could have with children who likely will encounter this book in public schools or libraries.

We learn at the end of the story that the little girl's first name, Alma, is all her own. Some astute readers may have already been wondering, or already know, what I am about to reveal next: Alma, in Spanish, means soul. "You are the first and only Alma," her father tells her. "I picked the name *Alma* just for you," he says, tweaking her nose as she laughs, and we see the family photo book resting alone on the chair. "I am Alma, and I have a story to tell," the book's concluding words read. We see Alma, the embodied little girl pictured in front of us, but we have been taken on a journey that is revealing to us, a story of her soul.

Catholic readers, of course, seeing the flower imagery throughout, will think of young St. Thérèse of Lisieux (1873–1897) and her famous Little Way, as recounted in her autobiography *Story of a Soul*. The Little Way of St. Thérèse of Lisieux is a spiritual path emphasizing doing small, everyday actions with great love and humility, trusting completely in God's grace. The child-saint writes in her autobiography, "God would never inspire me with desires which cannot be realized; so in spite of my littleness, I can hope to be a saint."[7] We see this aspiration of goodness, of inspiring within her a little way to create change in the world, in the story of Alma, too, the story of another soul.

On the final page, after Alma announces that she has a story to tell, we are presented with a picture of her in a photograph with the dove resting on her head and her eyes looking upward. For those who have the book, comparing Alma's picture at the end with the often-used photograph of St. Thérèse with the bun in her hair is useful. The picture of Alma is the same type of photograph that she is looking at and talking about as she discusses her names and those who inspired them in the photo book with her father. Alma may have *her* story to tell now, but it is a story she has connected not only to the past, but also to a destined future.

At some point, we can assume another little girl or boy will be asking a question similar to the one she asked her father, looking at this book with her in it, continuing a vibrant culture of life. The dove, placed above Alma's head and looking into her eyes, of course, reminds us that the story she writes is not her own, but it is guided by the Holy Spirit. Her eyes are lifted toward the dove, toward heaven, and the dove looks down, meeting her, body and soul, where she is. It is their story together, their communion story. The script of Alma's story is neither inside her, as we hear foretold in Disney's *Wish*, nor is it hers alone. Alma is not her own origin story. Her story is her family's and her community's. Beyond that, it is the story of the Holy Spirit at work in the world through her.

This sense of connection and continuity, from past to future, shapes the religious heart of the book. This heart might be symbolic, but it is not hidden by any means: We spot it on Alma's shirt throughout the book, the heart reminding readers of Mary's Immaculate Heart. The devotional practice Alma learns asks its adherents to take the fiery love of Jesus out into the world, to offer it to others. The book emphasizes that our identities are intertwined with those who came before us and those who will come after us, that we pass down what's in our hearts from one generation to the next. We offer God's love to others, and we pass down the spiritual, all "the things in memory," as Luke's Gospel reminds us, not simply the intellectual. It reaches and evangelizes the heart, answering the crisis of the church today. Juana Martinez-Neal's book is a powerful reminder of the enduring nature of family, faith, and the culture of life that binds us together if we open our

---

7. St. Thérèse of Lisieux, *My Catholic Life*.

hearts to it, even wearing them on our white T-shirts, as Alma does hers, for all to see.

Exploring *Little Women* by Louisa May Alcott (Ages Eight–Eighteen)

Alma and her family may be new to readers of this book, but I suspect most have heard, at least in passing, of Meg, Jo, Beth, and Amy March's family, even if they have not read Louisa May Alcott's classic *Little Women*. Alcott was raised by her Protestant philosopher parents, Bronson and Abigail Alcott, yet this book does have some specifically Catholic elements and alludes to others, which we discuss below. Scholars and fans have tried for years to figure out what ignited such fervor when this book was published and its staying power since then. Why have there been so many adaptations in the form of books, fan fiction, and other media?

And why, of all classics, do friends still discuss it with each other today, debating the romantic pairings of Jo with Professor Bhaer and Amy with Laurie, many still harboring anger that Amy burned Jo's manuscript pages when they were kids and feeling a lingering sadness over Beth's death from scarlet fever? Why do mothers pass down this book to their daughters or, as in a recent anecdote from one of my classes, grandmothers pass it down to their grandsons? Why does this book stay in print whereas other popular nineteenth-century books have disappeared from bookstore and library offerings? Sarah Chauncey Woolsey's *What Katy Did*, Susan Warner's *The Wide, Wide World*, and Martha Finley's Elsie Dinsmore series were all nineteenth-century bestsellers, and some of you may even recognize these titles, even love (or hate) some of the reading memories you have associated with them, but none of these books or series have retained the classic celebrity status of *Little Women*.

I am going to suggest a simple answer: *Little Women* has remained popular for over 150 years—and will continue to be so for years to come—because it celebrates a culture of life for women, young and old. It leans into a moral narrative about self-sacrificial love without apology and rings true to women's ideal expressions of life in community. In *The Afterlife of Little Women*, literary scholar Beverly Lyon Clark shares that when the novel was first published "the book was popular with boys as well as girls, and also with men and women: It struck a chord in the nineteenth-century U.S. imagination, as sales figures, library circulation records, fan letters, and personal testimony attest."[8] Since then, it has been most popular with women audiences, as they have shared it with each other, in families as mentioned above but also in shared friendships where the book has been a common link. *Little Women* has never been out of print, and it has been translated into more than fifty languages worldwide.[9] The book has also had seven different movie adaptations, twelve adaptations for US audiences alone, and a recent forty-eight-episode Japanese anime adaptation.[10]

My mother read it to me. My college students tell me stories of their mothers reading it to them. My friends and I of different generations, both older and younger, talk about it together. In a recent children's literature class I taught, a student discovered all of her mom's computer passwords were versions of the four daughters' names in *Little Women*. Her mother used these names because she remembered reading the book with her mother and with my student. The student only discovered this when interviewing her mother about the impact of the book for our class, and, though she remembered reading the book with her mother, she didn't know her grandmother had read it with her mom.

Little Women bristles with the importance of community, family, and the journey toward individual sanctification in thoughtful, committed relationship with others. It is unsurprising that sharing it with others one loves is the first impetus once one finishes the book or that its sharing transcends locations and generations.

In his 2013 apostolic exhortation *Evangelii Gaudium*, or "The Joy of Gospel," Pope Francis suggests that selfishness plagues humanity more than any other crisis. He writes,

> The great danger in today's world, pervaded as it is by consumerism, is the desolation and anguish born of a complacent yet covetous heart, the feverish pursuit of frivolous pleasures, and a blunted conscience. Whenever our interior life becomes caught up in its own interests and concerns, there is no longer room for others, no place for the poor. God's voice is no longer heard, the quiet joy of his love is no longer felt, and the desire to do good fades.[11]

Like Pope John Paul II, Pope Francis cautions about individual desires overtaking the joys of community and the culture of a life well lived together or

---

8. Clark, *Afterlife of Little Women*, 11.
9. Penguin Australia, "Classic of the Month: *Little Women*."
10. Smith, "How 'Little Women' Got Big."
11. Francis, *Evangelii Gaudium*.

a life dedicated to service to others instead of oneself. Like Jesus, we should treat love as self-gift.

Even in the very first chapter of *Little Women*, titled "Playing Pilgrims," when we are introduced to the March sisters at Christmastide, a setup between individual and community desires is conveyed, with communion being elevated as a good to be emulated. The four girls are asked by their mother, Marmee, to give up their meager breakfast pleasures for an even poorer family, the Hummels. Like most children, the girls initially resist this request. Yet, through their mother's example, they realize that sacrifice is exactly what Christmas calls for, and their hearts are transformed into love for others. What makes this story believable is that the transformation does not come without believable conversation, desire for bows over self-sacrifice, and lamentations over hardships.

The end of this first moral episode with the sisters concludes, however, with each daughter pledging to her mother, in her own way, that she will try to be less "frivolous" (I am pulling here from Pope Francis's exhortation) and try to act more like a Christian pilgrim. Their father is serving as a chaplain for the Union Army in the Civil War, and the daughters hope that by the time he returns they can be less "selfish." As Amy puts it after they all read a letter from their father aloud (note reading as an act of building a culture of life here): "I am a selfish girl! But I'll truly try to be better, so he mayn't be disappointed in me by and by."[12] "We all will!"[13] her sister Meg chimes in.

When introducing the book earlier, I mentioned the beginning proposition the book makes, that the four March sisters sacrifice their Christmas for the Hummels, a German-immigrant family who live in a run-down shack near the Marches. Right as they sit down to breakfast on Christmas morning, after having waited for an hour on their mother, who had been missing that morning from the family table, Marmee, the girls' mother, greets the children this way:

> Merry Christmas, little daughters! . . . I want to say one word before we sit down. Not far away from here lies a poor woman with a little new-born baby. Six children are huddled into bed to keep from freezing, for they have no fire. There is nothing to eat over there; and the oldest boy came to tell me they were suffering

---

12. Alcott, *Little Women*, 9.
13. Alcott, *Little Women*, 9.

hunger and cold. My girls, will you give them your breakfast as a Christmas present?[14]

The pressure the fictional March sisters must have felt! I feel it now, hearing Marmee's moving speech. What works in Alcott's book, though, and what is rare in fiction today, is the true reaction we have from the girls and that pull they, and we, have to be more like Marmee.

Importantly, the book's moral moving begins before we get to Marmee asking them this favor, with a scene of the girls fighting with each other. "'Christmas won't be Christmas without any presents,' grumble[s] Jo" is the iconic first line of the book, a line that begins with a complaint. The scene that follows not only reminds me of moments in my own house growing up with my family but also certainly captures a snapshot of my home life now with my children. The girls Alcott depicts are griping as they lie about the house, bemoaning their small selfish desires, especially in light of political unrest, the Civil War, that is happening around them.

They are not bad children, though: They are simply children. They are upset that they will not get presents during Christmas because of the war raging in the border states and that they, as children, are being asked to sacrifice something they naturally love—getting presents—for their neighbors and, by extension, for the country. On top of this great sacrifice, each girl believes she is having to give up more than the next one, and a game of who has it worse ensues: "'You don't have such a hard time as I do,' sa[ys] Jo," who complains about her job looking after a "fussy old lady."[15] In the book, Jo spends her days taking care of Aunt March and feels annoyed she cannot be in charge of what she wants to do with her time but instead must listen to, and wait upon, someone else.

On the other hand, Amy says she has it the worst because she has to go to school with "impertinent girls" who "label your father if he isn't rich."[16] Amy is more concerned at school about how she is perceived materially and socially than in getting an education. Each of the girls laments her lot being the worst and is quick to explain why. Yet the girls' complaining does not feel simpering or snotty: It feels like children dealing with the ups and downs of their lives. In fact, their culture clashes are not altogether different from today. Too often in stories, writers make children out as better or worse than they are. Alcott, however, shows children exactly as they are.

14. Alcott, *Little Women*, 13.
15. Alcott, *Little Women*, 4.
16. Alcott, *Little Women*, 13.

Culture of Life

They complain. They yell at each other. They want presents; they desire material things. Family life can be ideal at times, but, honestly, it often is not. It often is hard. As parents, caretakers, and educators, we should work to *inspire* a culture of life, not pretend it is always there or that it is always good. This is what Alcott does in *Little Women*: She inspires her characters, and her readers, to look beyond themselves, to find the good in their circumstances and in others, to inspire sanctification through community.

In *Evangelium Vitae*, Pope John Paul II writes that it was through envy and broken relationships that death first entered the world:

> The Gospel of life, proclaimed in the beginning when man was created in the image of God for a destiny of full and perfect life (cf. Gen 2:7; Wis 9:2–3), is contradicted by the painful experience of death which enters the world and casts its shadow of meaninglessness over man's entire existence. Death came into the world as a result of the devil's envy (cf. Gen 3:1,4–5) and the sin of our first parents (cf. Gen 2:17, 3:17–19). And death entered it in a violent way, through the killing of Abel by his brother Cain: "And when they were in the field, Cain rose up against his brother Abel, and killed him" (Gen 4:8).

When the March girls are complaining at the beginning of the story about not getting any presents, they are missing the point of Christmas altogether: celebrating Jesus's self-gift of love. We return to the idea of the incarnation, of Jesus bodily giving himself, taking on a human nature, to teach, heal, and save the world through his sacrificial love. Instead of starting out this way, instead of beginning with a Christmas story perfect in the manger, Alcott has the girls act sinfully like Cain, envying each other's stations and the stations of those around them.

Their mother, however, expects the best of them, and they want to act better, to embody the self-gift of love like Jesus, as she does, because they see Marmee doing this on Christmas morning, and we presume on most other days, too, giving her love to their little family and to those in need around them. The girls are each other's keepers, Alcott, through Marmee's modeling, conveys. This maxim is true in the March family and in the girls being seen as the keepers of their neighborhood as they care for the Hummels and the keepers of the United States as they are expected to sacrifice during the Civil War for the greater good, even if they grumble along the way.

After all, as much as they are complaining children, they are also children who respond after "only a minute,"[17] deciding that they would be glad to give their breakfast to a family that has none. The children Alcott depicts—the ones plagued with envy and selfishness, as we all are—do not give into their personal desires. They sacrifice willingly. It matters, too, that this sacrifice is bodily in nature. The girls will have "bread and milk" for breakfast but will not eat again, presumably, until "dinner-time."[18]

"'I thought you'd do it,' say[s] Mrs. March, smiling"[19] at them. In giving away their breakfast, we see the girls fasting on a holy day without announcing it or bemoaning it as they do other times. We see them become holy. We feel and witness the transformation of heart within the sisters. Denying themselves certain comforts brings the March sisters closer to God, and readers watch as the Hummels enjoy those comforts in front of them: The sacrifice is transferred from one to another without want on either side.

Fasting is not merely about abstaining from food; it is an act of penance, a way to purify the soul and strengthen the will against temptation. Fasting is a tangible way for the sisters to empathize with the suffering of others and to cultivate a spirit of generosity and compassion. Moreover, the theme of fasting connects to the broader narrative of self-discipline and moral fortitude found throughout the novel, especially when the characters are faced with various trials that test their resolve and character: Jo cutting her hair so her mother has money to rush off to take care of the father, who needs her because he is sick, is one example of this resolve. Another is Meg deciding not to marry for money even though she could because of her looks. These moments of struggle and sacrifice refine each of the girls' individual virtues while bonding them closer with their broader communities. In sacrificing, they are cultivating a culture that values life.

A Catholic reading of this novel, highlighting its promotion of a culture of life, ought to mention one other specific moment. When Beth is ill before the end of part 1, Hannah, a longtime family servant who has been charged with taking care of the girls while Marmee is in Washington taking care of Mr. March, after much coaxing from Meg and Jo decides to send Amy to live with her Aunt March while her sister gets better. There, Amy meets a French Catholic immigrant who is a servant of Aunt March's, and this woman comforts her. Had it not been for "the maid" at

---

17. Alcott, *Little Women*, 13.
18. Alcott, *Little Women*, 14.
19. Alcott, *Little Women*, 14.

her Aunt March's house, Amy would not "have got through that dreadful time. . . . Esther was a French woman. . . . Her real name was Estelle: but Aunt March ordered her to change it, and she obeyed on the condition that she never be asked to change her religion."[20] Anti-Catholic sentiment is a common feature in nineteenth-century fiction, but in Alcott's novel, the care with which Esther and her religiosity are introduced is unique. Alcott's own mother, Abba, worked with Irish Catholic immigrants as one of the first paid social workers in Boston. Though we do not know her specific thoughts about those experiences, we can infer from Alcott's inclusion of this scene in *Little Women* that she was open to some of the devotional practices at least, and it is worth pointing out to Catholic audiences when their faith is mentioned positively in the novel.[21]

While she is lonely and away from her nuclear family, Amy is attracted to her Aunt March's jewelry cabinet. Esther asks, as Amy stares and plays with the jewelry in the cabinet, "Which [piece] would Mademoiselle choose if she had her will?" Amy, "with great admiration," chooses "a string of gold and ebony beads, from which hung a heavy cross of the same." Amy has no idea what a rosary is, but she chooses it, seemingly attracted by its material charms. Esther says this would be her choice, too, but she clarifies that she "covets" that piece like "a good Catholic." She explains that "it would be pleasing to the saints if one used so fine a rosary as this, instead of using it as a vain bijou."[22]

As a "good Catholic," Esther wants the rosary to be used for its proper purpose, prayer. Amy, who has been characterized as struggling with worldliness more than any of the other March sisters, experiences for the first time a solemnity of the spirit. She reflects that Esther's own plain, wooden rosary beads lead her to worship joyfully and that she has never experienced such a spiritual feeling herself. While at her Aunt March's, she creates a prayer space in a closet, which even includes, like Alma, a devotion to "the divine Mother"[23] in the form of a beautiful picture that she gazes at as she prays. During these times, she prays "for dear God to preserve her sister," not a selfish prayer, but a prayer outward. Additionally, "[s]he tried to forget

20. Alcott, *Little Women*, 153.

21. For a deeper explanation of this moment in the novel, refer to another, and more extensive interpretation of this scene I wrote in "The Spiritual Life of Children During Pandemics."

22. Alcott, *Little Women*, 154.

23. Alcott, *Little Women*, 155.

herself, to keep cheerful, and be satisfied with doing right—though no one saw or praised her for it."[24] For Amy, devotion to Mary leads her to ponder and appreciate her relationship with Marmee, who, upon picking Amy up from her aunt's once Beth gets better, spends time in the space with her and praises her worship and journey toward selflessness.

Here, we come full circle and return to Pope John Paul II's words in *Evangelium Vitae*. When discussing the domestic church, the families of faith, where children like Amy and the others about whom readers of this book care and are reading to and with, he writes that the domestic church is "the love that becomes selflessness, receptiveness and gift. Within the family each member is accepted, respected and honoured precisely because he or she is a person; and if any family member is in greater need, the care which he or she receives is all the more intense and attentive."

In the tableaux of learning about the rosary and contemplative prayer, Amy discovers how to give up a little bit of selfishness, the main struggle we see her dealing with throughout the novel, so her sister who is sick can get the attention she needs. With this said, Marmee does not forget Amy. When she returns from Washington, Marmee visits Amy at her aunt's and listens attentively to her prayer journey when she meets with her. All the family members are accepted, and the love in the March household is shown repeatedly as selfless, as gift, even if the children within the story are imperfect, unique, and still forming. In *Little Women*, the relationships are fractured and real, yet the love and the domestic church ideal is worth every page, every tear, every heartfelt fulfilment, generation after generation.

A Reading Culture of Life

As adults who care about children's souls in today's world, we are all familiar with the increasing focus on individualism and "me culture." The act of reading with children may seem an unconventional clarion call to embrace and support Pope John Paul II's call to resist that me culture and to promote an outward culture of life instead. Yet reading together can work toward that goal in two ways.

First, in the act itself: Sitting with our children and concentrating on being present with them in the moment promotes a feeling of love and connection. Imagine the transformation to the domestic church, the parish home, and the school community if reading aloud, and discussing books

---

24. Alcott, *Little Women*, 155.

one reads by oneself in community afterward, were promoted as inherent goods in the world. As the psalmist declares in Psalm 133:1, "How good and pleasant it is when God's people live together in unity!" Fostering this communal spirit through shared reading practices nurtures bonds of empathy, understanding, and a deeper appreciation for the interconnectedness of all humanity. Simply reading and talking about books together is a good in and of itself.

Mem Fox's research here is important. Talking to and with children about books, and especially reading with them, is what develops their brains. Significantly, she relates that sitting with screens in no way has the same socio-emotional effect as reading aloud. "Television doesn't talk to children," she writes; "it talks at them and they can't talk back."[25] Likewise, religious educational programs teaching about doctrine or ideas do not have the same outcomes that reading with children does: You cannot build a culture of life through screens. You can through reading. In our day and age, it bears mention that there are a plethora of technologies that can mimic human relationships. Study after study has shown that reading aloud with a human is better for comprehension, though. No interactive technology beats a tangible book for teaching reading. When thinking about teaching spiritual practices, and building and thinking about a culture of life in particular, it stands to reason that humans are necessary to that process even more than teaching the ABCs.

Of course, this brings me to the second way that reading can be transformative in building a culture of life: Choose books that lead your children to make morally good choices. If you're choosing books that do not line up with Catholicism perfectly (unless you're reading the *Catechism* they probably don't), discuss that with them so they can discern religious morality in their lives. *Alma and How She Got Her Name* and *Little Women* are not perfectly Catholic books by any means, but they do foster main elements of the ideas of a culture of life.

In addition, consider the books you loved as a child, the books that made you want to be a better person, and bring them into your home, parish, library, or school. Try like Amy to build your own worship space or to be more spiritually attuned to the faith, for whatever reason and in whatever way rings truest to your domestic church, catechetical, or educational space. Likely the books you loved included some acts of self-sacrifice, family, and working together for a good moral outcome. Talk about heroes and

---

25. Fox, *Reading Magic*, 18.

heroines and their virtues, and talk about how those heroes and heroines are like Jesus, or not, even if the book doesn't explicitly make this connection. You are the expert when you are with a child or children you love. You are sacrificing your time in building that culture of life with them, so trust your judgment and enjoy reading books about this topic that speak to you. There are plenty of books referenced in the appendix of this book about a culture of life, but trust your judgment, too.

Build a reading culture of life around what you love. Your family. Your school. Your parish. Your children. Promote your culture of life with your children. As Alcott concludes in *Little Women*, "Love is a great beautifier."[26] Make the world more beautiful and more lively by reading together with those you love most.

Questions and Activity Ideas about *Alma and How She Got Her Name* and *Little Women*

Included below are questions to prompt meaningful discussions with your children. Each question is paired with an activity, providing parents with creative opportunities to strengthen the family's connection with the book's messages. *Alma and How She Got Her Name* questions and activities delve into family history, the meanings of names, and the importance of Catholic traditions, while *Little Women* ones prompt reflections on love, sacrifice, family unity, and virtues. The goal is to turn passive reading into an active, engaging experience. Find more book recommendations and related questions on building a culture of life in the appendix.

Alma and How She Got Her Name: Questions, with Activity Ideas

1. How does learning about the meanings of Alma's names remind you of God's love and plans for each of us?
    - **Activity:** Explore the meanings of your own name(s). Research together the saints, historical places, and/or biblical figures associated with those names. Draw a picture of you with your name and all its meanings!

---

26. Alcott, *Little Women*, 192.

2. Why do you think family history and traditions are important in Catholic families?

   - **Activity:** Create a family traditions scrapbook or journal. Include stories, pictures, and mementos that highlight important Catholic celebrations like Baptism and feast days that are important to you.

3. How does learning about your family and faith make you feel connected to God?

   - **Activity:** Plan a storytelling night focused on faith experiences with family or friends. Act out your favorite story with costumes you find in the house.

4. What is the Immaculate Heart of Mary? What can we learn about God's love for us through the Immaculate Heart of Mary?

   - **Activity:** Create an Immaculate Heart of Mary to hang up, using construction paper.

Little Women: Questions, with Activity Ideas

1. How does the March family show love and care for others, especially those less fortunate? What sacrifices do they make for each other and their community?

   - **Activity:** Volunteer together as a family or with friends at a local shelter or food pantry. Discuss how serving others reflects the March family's values of selflessness and compassion.

2. How do the various members of the March family support each other during difficult times, such as when Mr. March is away? What lessons can we learn about family unity and strength?

   - **Activity:** Plan a family or community night in which everyone shares a story about a time he or she supported others in the family. Create a "March Family Values" poster to display key lessons learned but substitute your family/group names.

3. How does the March family's faith guide their actions and decisions? How do they find strength in their beliefs during challenging moments?

- **Activity:** Attend Mass together and discuss how the readings or homily relate to themes of faith, perseverance, and hope as seen in *Little Women*.

4. How do the characters in *Little Women* grow and change? What virtues and struggles do they demonstrate? Which character has virtues that you would most like to emulate?

    - **Activity:** Choose a virtue (e.g., kindness, courage, humility) and create a challenge to practice it throughout the week, perhaps putting a button in a jar for every time you practice that virtue. Talk about the buttons you've accumulated at the end of the week. Share reflections on how practicing virtues can strengthen your family or community bonds and what you learned from the challenge.

4

Care of God's Creation in *The Snowy Day* and *The Wind in the Willows*

IT WOULD BE RARE to browse a children's section of a Catholic bookstore without finding quite a few picture books devoted to St. Francis of Assisi. Newbery Medal and National Book Award winner Katherine Paterson boasts one of the best. Her *Brother Sun, Sister Moon* was published in 2011 and is a gorgeous retelling of Assisi's 1224 hymn, the "Canticle of Creation." Directed toward children four to ten years old and illustrated by renowned cut-paper artist Pamela Dalton, the book is faithful to Catholic tradition while simultaneously illustrating why the tradition calls to children in a unique way. Children are often associated with St. Francis because of his love for nature, a love most famously expressed in his "Canticle of Creation," often also translated as "Canticle of the Sun" or "Canticle of the Creatures."[1]

Paterson begins her picture-book version of Assisi's prayer with the following words: "We come to sing a song of praise to you, O God, the Lord of Heaven and Earth, who by your power and out of your love have created all things and called them good."[2] St. Francis believed that all God's Earthly wonders ought to be treated with kindness and respect, whether those wonders be flowers, stars, twigs, or animals. By calling them "good," he invites humanity to recognize the deific presence within all living things and

---

1. Francis of Assisi, "Canticle of Creation."
2. All quotes come from Paterson, *Brother Sun, Sister Moon*.

the interconnectedness of life. God assigned us a "shared responsibility" to steward, or care for, his good gifts, with love and care.³

Like St. Francis, children have a natural affinity for nature, hence the popularity of books about this saint in every Catholic bookstore. For instance, consider the common association of children with playing outdoors. One aspect of the school day my children look forward to most is recess, because they get to roam outside. Picking dandelions, climbing trees, and swinging on playsets underneath bright blue skies is a highlight not just of their school days but of all days. One cherished activity my daughter often speaks of, and that I remember from my own childhood, is searching for caterpillars, ladybugs, and butterflies on the playground. As a child, I remember waiting patiently for caterpillars to crawl on my fingers, inching toward the back of my hand and up my arm. I giggled at the fuzziness of the creature's many legs and marveled at how this long, wormlike being could metamorphosize into a lovely butterfly by summer's end.

Eric Carle's picture book *The Very Hungry Caterpillar* was always a childhood favorite of mine and is a favorite of my children, who are likewise inspired by the vibrant colors within the story, not to mention the glory of God's creation it proclaims. As Christian readers of the story, we need only to evoke the obvious sacred beauty within the book. If we'd like to take our discussion a step further when speaking with young children, we might even compare the caterpillar to Jesus who emerged, resurrected from the tomb—as the caterpillar does from his cocoon—transformed into a new, mysterious, and wondrous life that gives hope to those who read and hear this story about him.

Additionally, like St. Francis, and the famous iconography of him, most children are drawn to animals and to stories featuring them, like Carle's famous one about the voracious caterpillar.⁴ It is our responsibility

---

3. Francis, *Laudato Si'*.

4. In Catholic educational circles, the Catechesis of the Good Shepherd is one way children's natural attunement to animals is used in a parish setting to teach a Christ-centered, or christological, approach to Catholic teaching and liturgy. Introduced by Sofia Cavaletti in 1954, this approach draws upon the parable of the good shepherd (John 10:3–5, 11–16) as a base. In this parable, Jesus describes himself as the "good shepherd" who guides his sheep through a gate. The sheep recognize their shepherd's voice and follow him, but they will not follow a stranger. The good shepherd leads his sheep to green pastures and provides for their needs. He knows his sheep by name and cares for them deeply, even risking his own life to protect them from harm. Through this parable, Jesus contrasts himself with hired hands who do not care for the sheep as he does, emphasizing the loving and protective presence of Jesus for each of us, his sheep. When catechizing

as children's caretakers to guide their natural inclinations—to invite sacred interpretations of real-life experiences and offer interpretations of literature about similar experiences that benefit the common good. Perhaps it goes without saying that there is no statue or form as easily recognizable by children and adults alike as that of St. Francis, whose likeness is often flocked (pun intended) on all sides by chickens, rabbits, deer, and other animals. At my local parish and others, I often see children gazing at St. Francis's image more than those of the other saints, their eyes lingering at a sheep resting at his feet or a dove perched on his outstretched hand.

Ceremonial blessings of the animals are popular at parishes and Catholic schools on St. Francis's Feast Day (October 4), as they signify the love we humans have for the creatures God entrusted us to tend (Gen 1:28). Through the nurturing of pets, children often first learn to cultivate a reverence for God's creation, especially one in which they have an explicit shared responsibility to contribute.[5] A plethora of picture books and chapter books explore the theme of children desiring pets to love and care for, including picture books such as *The Pigeon Wants a Puppy!*, by Mo Willems (ages two to eight), *Lola Gets a Cat*, by Anna McQuinn (ages two to nine), and *Toby*, by Hazel Mitchel (ages two to eight), as well as chapter books like *Charlotte's Web*, by E. B. White (ages six to twelve), *Where the Red Fern Grows*, by Wilson Rawls (ages nine to fourteen), and *Because of Winn-Dixie*, by Kate DiCamillo (ages seven to thirteen).

Pope Francis's encyclical *Laudato Si'* ("Praised Be") takes its name from a line in his "Canticle of Creation." The encyclical suggests we all ought to strive to preserve the wonder children naturally have for God's creation. If God has created all things and "called them good," as St. Francis articulates in his "Canticle," then it follows that as adults we ought to make a concerted effort to appreciate that good intentionally and both praise and encourage our children when they do so. Alongside our children, we ought to wonder at the good. We ought to spend more time letting caterpillars crawl up our

---

with this approach, the passage from the Bible is read and children are provided materials (animal figures, etc.) to reenact the story. They are also invited to create art and to meditate in an "atrium," or devoted space, created for this type of worship. I suggest that one reason, among many, why this catechetical approach is so successful is because it calls upon children's innate care for God's creation and love for animals. Literature can be another way to harness children's natural tendencies and interests to encourage worship, relationships, and liturgical understanding.

5. Francis, *Laudato Si'*.

arms and listen to our children's stories when they tell us about those seemingly small, yet no less sacramental, or grace-filled, moments.

Pope Francis puts it this way in *Laudato Si'*:

> Inner peace is closely related to care for ecology and for the common good because, lived out authentically, it is reflected in a balanced lifestyle together with a capacity for wonder which takes us to a deeper understanding of life. Nature is filled with words of love, but how can we listen to them amid constant noise, interminable and nerve-wracking distractions, or the cult of appearances? Many people today sense a profound imbalance which drives them to frenetic activity and makes them feel busy, in a constant hurry which in turn leads them to ride rough-shod over everything around them.

I quote this whole passage because it frames care for God's creation in a way that children are predisposed to understand, live out, and even teach to the adults with whom they interact and live. Young children under the age of ten especially tend to stop what they are doing and engage any or all of their senses with the wonders of creation around them. They gaze, touch, smell, listen, and even taste the elements of the world in their midst. How many of us remember the way dirt looks, feels, smells, sounds, and even tastes from when we were playing as children or washing our children's clothes as adults?

Beyond sensing the natural world, children will also ask *why* the world works as it does, over and over. *Why* do bees make honey? *Why* does rain fall and form puddles to splash in? *Why* does grass stain shorts green? *Why* can birds fly when I cannot? *Why* does the breeze on my arms make the hair stand up? The "constant noise" of our lives, our smartphones and our computers, might entice us as caretakers to Google the answers to questions like these when we ought first to sing God's praises with our children and revel at the bounty of riches in the world.

God is the reason for the *why*. In our busyness, we often forget to recognize these queries, and the wonderment that inspired them, as riches in and of themselves, as products of our children's natural wonder. We answer questions routinely, even absently, rather than joining in on the awe children feel that leads them to search together for "a deeper understanding of life." This does not mean that every time a child asks a question we should feel pressure to respond in some grand theological manner or to be perfect spiritually or emotionally. Instead, it is a call, like all our faith, to try to remember to put faith in the center of our lives, even in these small moments when we might not immediately recognize its central place.

As mentioned in the faith and reason chapter, centering faith does not mean we neglect the scientific *why* of children's queries. However, it does mean we take time to sink into the wonder that they feel for the big and small details of God's plan as they see it unfolding in the world. It means we recognize and point out the details of that plan as such. Psalm 139:14 reminds us to praise God because his "works are wonderful" and we "know that full well." Likewise, Pope Francis reminds us in his encyclical to remember to "listen" to the "words of love" in nature, to listen to what God reveals to us through his creation.

As parents, teachers, and educators, we can resist the "profound imbalance" of "frenetic activity" that can leads to us forgetting that we know "full well" how "wonderful" God's creation is, whether it means forgetting to make time to care for nature, animals, or our human brothers and sisters. Our children instinctively make time: They have a "balanced capacity of wonder." We should not be the ones to mar their wonder with our adult "imbalance." Rather, we should provide them with models of how to retain their wonder and harness it into a thoughtful stewardship of the natural world.

This brings us full circle to St. Francis's hymn. In her translation of his "Canticle," Paterson concludes *Brother Sun, Sister Moon* with these words: "We praise you," God, "[f]or all of your gifts—for this wondrous universe in which we live, for family, for friends, for work and play, for this life and the life to come—we sing our praise to you." Here, the focus is on the union of wonder and balance, work and play, this life and the next. Often, when speaking of how to care for the Earth, we look outside of ourselves to what we cannot control. Perhaps one day the children we guide will lead systemic changes in corporations and governments. Most of us will not sit in those positions of high-level power, though. As a starting point to wherever our children may venture forth in the future, we can begin their journeys toward caring for the Earth with what most of them can control now no matter their starting points—balancing their lives and maintaining their sense of awe at the natural world.

In *The Grace of Enough: Pursuing Less and Living More in a Throwaway Culture*, popular Catholic children's writer and podcaster Haley Stewart relates that care of creation "require[s] intentionality, sacrifice, and attention in a world that prioritizes selfishness, convenience, and distraction. Such a reorientation honors God's design for human beings, their relationship with each other, and his world."[6] As caregivers to children and the world at large, the latter is what we can focus on as we read books about nature's wonders. How can we reorient our children, and ourselves for that matter, to honor God's designs for our relationships? Reading with children in and of itself, I suggest, is a relationship that is part of God's design and one that ought to be focused on worship. As a practice, it helps not only to talk about wonder, but to nourish it through relationship.

This chapter will explore two classic books, *The Snowy Day* (ages two to eight), Ezra Jack Keats's classic 1962 picture book, and *The Wind in the Willows* (ages eight to fourteen), Kenneth Grahame's 1908 chapter book. The latter is considered a chapter book based on length and target audience, yet it is still widely beloved by older (and perhaps younger) audiences for its beautiful pictures, originally provided by Ernest Shepard, who was commissioned for the project because of his previous success with the artwork for A. A. Milne's Winnie-the-Pooh series. *The Wind in the Willows*, as an illustrated chapter book, has been chosen for this chapter in part because it is attentive to multiple sensory dimensions, and many of the best chapter books older audiences may use to discuss care for God's creation will have illustrations, including all of the chapter books mentioned above.

The Snowy Day and *The Wind in the Willows* inspire readers to foster an intentional, grateful disposition toward creation. Similar to many of the other children's texts this book covers, they are used in a variety of familial and educational settings. More than that, though, each text uniquely invites its child readers—and the adults who care for them—to journey to God-enchanted landscapes. The stories tell of wonder as readers build a relationship through nature tales, creating and restoring a relationship with nature that was disrupted from the beginning of humankind's relationship with God, depicted in the book of Genesis.

Pope Francis writes in *Laudato Si'* that "human life is grounded in three fundamental and closely intertwined relationships: with God, with our neighbour, and with the earth itself. According to the Bible, these three vital relationships have been broken, both outwardly and within us. This rupture is sin."[7] Because humans tried to take God's place in the creation story and did not care for the Earth or each other, we lost the harmonious balance God hoped for our world and our lives in it (Gen 1:28; 3:17–19).

---

6. Stewart, *Grace of Enough*, 37.
7. Francis, *Laudato Si'*.

We can help to restore and to heal the rupture we created by building relationships with God, each other, and the natural world he directed us to steward. I believe that through building a culture of reading with our children—one that models a vital and healthy relationship bond that honors and intentionally teases out the implicit wonder and awe children already have for nature—we can help to heal the wounds caused by humankind's selfishness both in the garden of Eden and in the days, years, and generations thereafter. Together, we can form a new generation modeled more like St. Francis, bonded rightly as he was with God, neighbor, and the Earth.

Exploring *The Snowy Day* by Ezra Jack Keats (Ages Two–Eight)

Living in San Antonio, Texas, every winter my children dream of snow: what it might be like to make snow angels, build snowmen, throw snowballs, and simply feel the cold flakes on their noses. Although they have experienced snow twice now since they have been born—which my daughter attributes wholly to her prayers—it is a rare occasion for our family. Hence, I should not have been surprised when, one morning, my then-kindergarten-aged daughter asked if she could watch an animated storybook that her class had recently seen about Ezra Jack Keats's *The Snowy Day*. While we were watching it together, I recalled being enchanted by the same story as a child, and while watching it I was swept up again by the wonder of the tale. Later that week we went to the library together and checked out a copy of the book, excited to share the picture-book experience that way, too.

The Snowy Day won the Caldecott Medal in 1963. As you might already have known or might recall from reading in the last chapter about another Caldecott award winner, *Alma and How She Got Her Name*, the Caldecott is an award given by the American Library Association for the year's children's book with the best illustrations. *The Snowy Day* was the first book featuring a Black child protagonist to receive the honor. Keats, who illustrated as well as wrote the book, was celebrated for his vibrant color palette and unique collage techniques. One aspect of *The Snowy Day* I especially appreciate is that it is not a pastoral story in the traditional sense. However, it still hearkens to that genre.

Most pastoral stories, including *The Wind in the Willows*, which we will speak about in a moment, are illustrated with soft, impressionistic, forest colors. *The Snowy Day* is brightly hued with gray undertones, yet its readers leave feeling no less pastorally inspired.

Stated simply, in literary terms, pastoral tales are those that portray nature: They are usually focused on country life and rural settings. *The Snowy Day*, on the other hand, offers an urban environment, inspired by Keats's childhood in Brooklyn. Because the boy protagonist, Peter, focuses on nature around his city neighborhood, we witness him restoring order to his own pastoral world. This restoration of the pastoral is where the sacramental grace—the grace of the Holy Spirit—is found in this text.

The term "pastoral," both in how we use it in literature and the way we use it in the church as a term of ministry, is derived from the Latin "pastor," meaning "shepherd." Jesus, of course, is known as the Good Shepherd, the one who looks after us humans, his flock (John 10:11, 10:14). If we are restoring right-ordered thinking in our children, and ourselves, then we can witness how our busy, disordered lives can be made better if we pause our "constant hurry" and pay attention to nature, as Peter does in the story.[8]

The book begins with a picture of a boy gazing out of his window, looking at snow "as far as he could see." He dons a bright red snowsuit, leaves the house, makes different types of tracks in the snow, finds a stick buried beneath it, and beats a snow-laden tree with that stick. "Down fell the snow—PLOP!—on top of Peter's head," we read.[9] The pictures show him from afar hitting the tree with the stick, then up close as the snow falls on his head, and finally from afar again as he wanders away and makes new tracks in the snow and moves toward new adventures. Note the sensory details already in the story. Peter gazes, grabs, and listens (PLOP!). We also witness globs of snow sliding down his bright red snowsuit hat, knowing that he tastes and feels the cold of the snow, too.

The snow also invites him to imagine new ways of being, to pretend he's "a mountain-climber!" Importantly, his imagination is not prideful but rather meant for play: He slides down a large hill. While he imagines he is a mountain-climber, he knows he is not quite one yet. There is likewise no evidence that this is a lifelong dream of his, only that the snow, that nature, inspires imaginative thinking.

Indeed, Peter has a recognition of self that is healthy. Keats writes that Peter "thought it would be fun to join the big group of boys in their snowball fight, but he knew he wasn't old enough—not yet." In Genesis, we

8. Francis, *Laudato Si'*.
9. Keats, *Snowy Day*.

might recall that one of the ways humans rupture their relationship with God, each other, and the Earth (what Pope Francis calls those "three fundamental and intertwined relationships") is because they desire to be like God when they cannot be. When Adam and Eve decide to eat of the Tree of Knowledge of Good and Evil, they want to acquire God's understanding. This sin of pride is how the serpent tempts them both. He tells Eve, "For God knows that when you eat from [the tree] your eyes will be opened, and you will be like God, knowing good and evil" (Gen 3:5).

In Keats's story, Peter wants to join the older boys, but he realizes he is not like them, at least "not yet." Rather than being prideful or sulking, he decides to build "a smiling snowman" and "he made angels." It feels pertinent to mention that Peter bears the name of the biblical disciple Peter, who learned about his place and right relationship in the church through his friendship with Jesus. Peter in *The Snowy Day* does not grumble about who he is not but accepts who he is. He is not an older boy, but a younger one. He enjoys the activities he can do as a younger boy. He accepts his place in the world and appreciates it.

Once he arrives home, we see him again experiencing a relationship that is loving and right-ordered, his relationship with his mother. Keats writes that Peter walked into his house and "told his mother all about his adventures while she took off his wet socks." Peter allows himself to be nurtured, and he shares his love of nature with his mother as she cares for him. In the New Testament, washing someone's else's feet symbolizes humility, a trait Peter shows throughout this story because he is quick to accept his place in the world. Similarly, we see Peter's mother modeling humility. As his mother, she could tell Peter to wash his feet himself.

After all, we just saw Peter walk around the neighborhood without help, so we can assume he can wash his own feet. Instead, she *chooses* to wash Peter's feet and listens as he regales her with his adventures in the snow. Catholic readers might remember that Jesus washed the feet of the disciples during the Last Supper, including those of his disciple Peter (John 13:1–17). In washing his disciples' feet, an act usually reserved for the lowliest of servants, Jesus as leader exemplified sacrificial love for his followers. This gesture foreshadowed Jesus's humbling of himself in the crucifixion: In allowing himself to be humiliated, tortured, and crucified by humanity, Jesus demonstrated the depth of his love and his commitment to redeeming the world. Through his death and resurrection, Jesus offered salvation to all who believe in him, fulfilling the salvific promise of Christianity and inviting believers into a right relationship of grace with him.[10]

Importantly, in the book, we see Peter accepting the role God has given him in life and choosing right relationships repeatedly. He shares with his mother how he has nurtured the world by enjoying its beauty and wondering at it. Then she, as his mother and caretaker, encourages his awe and exhibits sacrificial love by washing his feet and listening to him. The order of creator-neighbor-Earth is upheld in *The Snowy Day* as an ideal. Peter gazes and then ventures into God's world (Creator), tells his mother what he experienced (neighbor) about the Creator's glory, and together they praise the Earth all while cultivating their loving bond. The relationships we see in this story—between young boy and older boys, between Peter and nature, between mother and son—are reciprocal and right-ordered. They support what Pope Francis in *Laudato Si'* terms an integral ecology, a relationship between humans and the Earth that is interrelated and dependent on supporting each other.

Next in the story is one of the most important parts for Catholics who care about the contemplative life. Keats shows Peter in the tub, by himself. After he has relayed his adventures to his mother, Peter "thought and thought and thought about them." Peter, while becoming clean physically and perhaps symbolically through the cleansing water, contemplates, or thinks about his excursions in nature and his relationship to the world outside. Now, the book does not say Peter prays here, but prayer and meditation take many forms, especially for children, and this moment provides an opportunity to speak to children about the differences and similarities between *thinking* and *praying*.

Thinking about our adventures *is* a form of prayer if we direct it as praise to God. If God is not a part of the thinking, then it is not prayer. Do the children we are reading with believe Peter thanks God for his snowy adventures when he is in the bathtub? Could he pray and think in the bathtub? Is it possible to do both? What is the difference between thinking and praying exactly as our children understand it? Child readers can examine the picture of Peter in the bathtub, determine whether Peter's eyes are open or closed, and consider whether they think their eyes can be open and/or closed during prayer. Even the illustrated bubbles arising out of the bathtub

---

10. Beyond the salvific imagery of Christ washing his disciples' feet and demonstrating sacrificial love, the image of Peter's mother washing his feet as he tells her about his day in the snow is reminiscent of Marian iconography in the Catholic faith.

in the picture with Peter look like "thought bubbles" and can be used as illustrations for what children might believe Peter is either thanking God for or what they might thank God for after enjoying a snowy day.

The book concludes with Peter falling sleep, dreaming of snow, of worrying about it melting. Will the enchantment snow brings to the world be there the next day? When he wakes up, new snow is falling, and Peter acts as we all should when we see God's glory in nature. He raises his hands high in the air, in a praise position, and we see the exclamation, "New snow was falling!" What else does Peter do? For those who know of St. Peter's exemplary life as a missionary, church builder, and first pope, it will come as no surprise. The child-protagonist Peter in the story "calls to his friend from across the hall and they [go] out together into the deep, deep snow." Like St. Peter, the child shares the good news of the snow. He proclaims the good news of God's creation with others whom he loves. All of our children, and all of us, can and ought, I would argue, to follow this boy's grace-filled, loving example and build their own relationships with God, their neighbors, and the Earth.

Exploring *The Wind in the Willows* by Kenneth Grahame (Ages Eight–Fourteen)

As mentioned above, *The Snowy Day* can be considered an urban pastoral story. *The Wind in the Willows*, however, is perhaps one of the most well-known and beloved traditional pastoral stories ever conceived and composed. Like many children's tales that can be used to discuss care for God's creation, its main characters are animals, in this case Mole, Rat, Badger, and Toad. Following their marriage in 1899, Kenneth Grahame and his wife, Elspeth, had a son, Alistair, whom they nicknamed "Mouse."[11] He was born prematurely, was a small child, and suffered health ailments his entire life. In building a relationship with his son, Grahame told Alistair bedtime stories, and while away from his family on holiday, Grahame sent home detailed letters about the adventures of the animals in his stories. His wife encouraged him to compile the stories into what would later become *The Wind in the Willows*, a tale famously treasured by President Theodore

---

11. Brody, *Biography of Kenneth Grahame*. All biographical information about Grahame comes from this source.

Roosevelt and now issued in over one hundred editions, with yearly sales still numbering into the hundreds of thousands.[12]

As a basic sketch, the book follows Mole, Rat, Badger, and Toad as they navigate the idyllic English countryside together. It begins with Mole's decision to leave his underground home to explore the River Bank. There, he meets Rat, and the two embark on various escapades together. The plot sounds simple, benign even, but there's a reason this book was an instant bestseller and has remained beloved to this day: It captures the interconnected world of relationships and nature—depicting both as wondrous and deserving of awe. Let us begin with Grahame's description of Mole's encountering the River Bank, which he describes as "too good to be true." Mole

> thought his happiness was complete when, as he meandered aimlessly along, suddenly he stood by the edge of a full-fed river. Never in his life had he seen a river before—this sleek, sinuous, full-bodied animal, chasing, and chuckling, gripping things with a gurgle and leaving them with a laugh, to fling on fresh playmates that shook themselves free, and were caught and held again. All was a-shake and a-shiver—glints and gleams and sparkle, rustle and swirl, chatter and bubble. The mole was bewitched, entranced, fascinated.[13]

Like Peter in *The Snowy Day*, Mole has nowhere else to be, and no one else to be but who he is. He pauses, "suddenly" awe-filled it seems, and experiences what Pope Francis describes in *Laudato Si'* as peace," a moment "lived out authentically." Multiple senses are engaged: He stares, listens to, and feels the water. The moment is not only physically but also spiritually sensual. It is a moment of transcendence. He is "entranced" and "fascinated." Experiencing awe at the river has moved him beyond the physical to the sacramental. Catholics believe God speaks through the things God created to reveal himself. This means that all things shine with the splendor of God's grace: The invisible world is greater, richer, and larger than the visible. Mole, as he encounters the "too good to be true" River Bank, sees into this other, invisible world.

Recalling again Pope Francis's words in *Laudato Si'*, the River Bank's beauty transports Mole to "a deeper understanding of life." I have shared here only one poetic passage from the text that describes the pastoral world, but Grahame's writing is filled with aesthetically beautiful descriptions. It is no accident that at least fifty artists have illustrated this book since it was

---

12. Kamiya, "*Wind in the Willows* Celebrates a Century."
13. Grahame, *Wind in the Willows*, 3–4.

Care of God's Creation

first written. They, too, are inspired by Grahame's words and want to depict the images in different visual ways. In fact, a 2010 edition of the book illustrated by artist Inga Moore has sold over 100 million copies.[14]

Grahame's words enchant readers because they invite an unhurried approach to life, one perfect for visual artists seeking to be moved toward a closer relationship with nature and what it signifies. When describing the relationship between God, nature, and artists, French philosopher Jacques Maritain once stated that God "is beauty itself, because He gives beauty to all created beings."[15] Visual artists keep coming back to Grahame's story, inspired to recreate the adventures of the animals within it, because they are inspired by the healing occurring in it and can take part in that healing by depicting the images they find in Grahame's words.

Indeed, when reading the book with children, lingering and gazing alongside Mole at the River Bank depicted by whatever illustrator was inspired to create the pictures that you are reading together is significant. Dwell on the details. Converse about what colors are used, what the flowers might smell like, how cool the water might feel to the touch, and whether child readers imagine the setting looks as it is depicted. If not, what is missing? What could be added? What is already perfect? The glasses sitting on Mole's nose are ones my children found perfect when we discussed this book's details.

The glasses balance Moles's long face, with their round rims, allowing him to see in new ways (like a symbol, my son said!). Plus, they seem cool, glassy, and hard to the touch and, again, provide a balance to the warm and soft mole, whose personality seemed interested in streams and in reflections that he could see only with help from these glasses. Invite children's imaginations not only into the words of this story but also into the images because the relationship between word and image, and the shared imagining between child and adult when discussing Grahame's descriptions of the natural world, make this book particularly resonant.

As much as the story is about nature, it is about relationships, which is another reason the book feels especially conducive to being read aloud. Each of the four animals described throughout Grahame's book are unique. They are quirky, funny, adorable, and, sometimes, like family, friends, and parishioners, they get on each other's nerves. Like all of the aforementioned, they do and say the wrong things. They sin. Mole becomes jealous of Rat

14. Carey, "Inga Moore."
15. Maritain, *Art and Scholasticism*.

because "pride" whispers to him. He becomes convinced he can navigate a boat just as well as his new friend can even though he visited the River Bank for the first time only that day: We read above about how enchanted he was by the river. Mole had never been on a boat, yet he is jealous that Rat, who has lived there for years and has used a boat any times, is adept at handling the vessel. As happens in the garden of Eden, Mole disrupts the beautiful serenity he had appreciated and expressed awe for earlier in the day. Later, when Rat took him on the boat tour, he

> jumped up and seized the sculls so suddenly, that the Rat, who was gazing out over the water and saying more poetry-things to himself, was taken by surprise and fell backwards off his seat with his legs in the air . . . while the triumphant Mole took his place and grabbed the sculls with entire confidence.[16]

Mole capsizes the boat! He flings himself, and his friend, into the water. Metaphorically, we see Eden being ruptured with the sin of pride again. Yet Grahame reminds his child and adult readers that they can help to heal the rupture of humanity's fallen nature through forgiveness and, yes, even through laughter, which Rat heartily engages in after assessing his own "drowned rat" state and his new friend's bravado and excitement about his abilities to navigate the river.

As we all ought to do when we sin, Mole quickly asks for forgiveness, realizing his wrongdoing. "Ratty, my generous friend, I am very sorry," he says. "Will you overlook it this once and forgive me, and let things go on as before?" Ratty not only agrees but also "bless[es]" his friend. Grahame's world is restored to goodness through friendship, forgiveness, blessing, and shared appreciation of nature. It is restored through the world being ordered right again. Grahame ends the first chapter of this "pastoral" tale, a tale of the countryside and of ministry, this way: Mole "learnt to swim and to row, and entered into the joy of running water; and with his ear to the reed-stems he caught, at intervals, something of what the wind went whispering so constantly among them."[17] Mole learns to catch the whispered "words of love" that Pope Francis says we ought to listen for in nature but often cannot hear because our lives are filled with "constant noise, interminable and nerve-wracking distractions." If we pause and put our ears to "the reed-stems," the

---

16. Grahame, *Wind in the Willows*, 18–19.
17. Grahame, *Wind in the Willows*, 23.

"words of love" are what *The Wind in the Willows* offers to us. We simply must open ourselves, and the children we read with, to the whispers.[18]

Learning to Care for God's Creation through Reading

Considering the difference between secular and Christian writers, children's author Madeleine L'Engle once stated: "Coming home. That's what it's all about. The journey to the coming of the kingdom. That's probably the chief difference between the Christian and the secular artist—the purpose of the work, be it story or music or painting, is to further the coming of the kingdom, to make us aware of our status as children of God, and to turn our feet toward home."[19] I suggest that the difference between the secular and the Christian reader is the same. When we read with children, our goal ought to be to lead to the kingdom, to turn their feet toward God. When discussing the natural world, what is fascinating is that the relationship works both ways. When we read together, we direct children's reading toward God, but their gazes direct ours. The act of reading in and of itself potentially becomes sacramental and grace-filled.

In the pages of *The Snowy Day* and *The Wind in the Willows*, we witness the unfolding of this reciprocal relationship between nature, literature, and spirituality. We witness Pope Francis's call for an interrelated view of care for God's creation. These stories provide fertile ground for nurturing a Catholic perspective on the wonders of the natural world. While the focus here is on these particular tales, I encourage you to extend this pastoral perspective to other stories that resonate within your family, school, or parish community. The healing of the world and the exploration of creation narratives are as simple as the resounding refrain of his "Canticle of Creation": "Praised be!" Seek those moments in any story you share with the children in your care, and therein lies a sacred opportunity to celebrate and honor the beauty of God's creation.

---

18. Francis, *Laudato Si'*.
19. L'Engle, *Walking on Water*.

Wondrous Reading

Questions and Activity Ideas about *The Snowy Day* and *The Wind in the Willows*

Included below are questions to prompt meaningful discussions. Each question is paired with an activity, providing creative opportunities to strengthen connections with the book's messages. *The Snowy Day* questions and activities look at the wonders of winter, exploring how the natural world reveals God's design. *The Wind in the Willows* questions focus on friendship, loyalty, and stewardship of the natural world. The goal is to turn passive reading into an active, engaging experience. Find more book recommendations and related questions on the care of God's creation in the appendix.

The Snowy Day: Questions, with Activity Ideas

1. What signs of God's creation can you find in the snow?
   - **Activity:** Take a nature walk with your child(ren) and collect small leaves or twigs. Create a simple "Thank You, God" card with these natural materials and place it in a windowpane for God to see.

2. Have you ever noticed that no two snowflakes look the same? Why do you think that is?
   - **Activity:** Create snowflakes by painting round coffee filters with blue watercolor paint and adding glitter for sparkle. Once dry, punch a hole at the top and hang with string to decorate your home with wintry beauty.

3. Why is it important to notice how pretty nature is? What do you like most about nature?
   - **Activity:** Take a walk outside and see how many different things you can find that show how God cares for his creation. Notice anything particular to the season, such as icicles, leaves, or flowers.

4. What's your favorite nature word or picture in a story about nature?
   - **Activity:** Start a nature journal to write or draw pictures about things outside. Make sure to connect the writings or pictures to God in some way! Let your imagination flow.

Care of God's Creation

Wind in the Willows: Questions, with Activity Ideas

1. How do the themes of friendship and loyalty in *The Wind in the Willows* reflect the Christian value of loving one another as Christ loves us? How do our relationships with each other relate to care of God's creation?

    - **Activity**: Host a *The Wind in the Willows* read-aloud with friends or family. Read one chapter and then print out or have available Proverbs 17:17 and John 15:13. Discuss how these verses relate to the friendships depicted in the book.

2. How does the beauty of nature depicted in *The Wind in the Willows* remind us of God's creation and his presence in the world around us? What's the loveliest area in your neighborhood that helps you to think of God?

    - **Activity**: Organize a prayer walk in a local park or nature reserve. As you walk, pause to reflect on the sights, sounds, and smells of nature and offer prayers of thanksgiving for God's creation.

3. Read one of your favorite passages from *The Wind in the Willows* aloud that focuses on a beautiful, outdoor place. How does *The Wind in the Willows* inspire us to steward God's creation and appreciate the wonders of the natural world as gifts from him?

    - **Activity**: Participate in a conservation project, such as planting trees or cleaning up a local waterway, as a way of caring for God's creation. Reflect on how your efforts align with God's command to be stewards of the Earth.

4. What role does adventure play in the lives of the characters in *The Wind in the Willows*? How do they handle challenges and obstacles they encounter in a Christian way? How is nature tied with adventure and awe?

    - **Activity**: Plan an outdoor adventure with friends, such as hiking, biking, or camping. Discuss the challenges you face in planning and brainstorm creative solutions, just as the characters in the book do.

Epilogue

Reading Wondrously

THIS PAST SUMMER, MY family and I took a vacation to the Grand Canyon. I hadn't expected to feel the awe that I did in that space. The vastness and beauty almost brought me to tears: I didn't want to leave. My family prayed there, and we talked about God's brushstrokes in creating the vibrancy of the world. Our hearts, and our souls, were moved.

As we were leaving a museum room in the Grand Canyon park, my husband noticed a quote on the wall from American writer and poet Carl Sandburg that he remarked spoke to him. We went to grab a picture with our phones of it, imagining that we might hang it somewhere in our house alongside a picture of the canyon itself. "Each man sees himself in the Grand Canyon," the quote read on the sand-colored wall, "each one makes his own Canyon before he comes, each one brings and carries away his own Canyon."[1] We began to talk about what we were carrying from this trip when my elementary-school-aged daughter said, "I have a favorite quote, too. It's from *Charlotte's Web*."

Here's the thing: my daughter has never been asked, nor forced, to memorize any passages from *Charlotte's Web*. Although our family reads together often (as you can tell from the contents of this book), she does not consider herself a reader. Nor does she often get the highest marks in school for her reading skills. Thus, we were a little shocked when she shared, without pausing, this quote from E. B. White's *Charlotte's Web*: "You have been my friend. That is the greatest gift I could ever receive." Now, connoisseurs of *Charlotte's Web* will know that my daughter repeated this

---

1. Sandburg, "Many Hats," 434.

quote wrong, and still does to this day. The correct quote is this: "You have been my friend. That in and of itself is a tremendous thing."[2]

When I asked her about how she learned the quote, she told me she read that passage aloud over and over to herself and then repeated it under her breath. Basically, because she liked it so much, she memorized it on her own. Her young mind and ears processed and heard the words about the gift being received rather than the "tremendous thing in and of itself," an error I find lovely rather than objectionable. The words, to me, express nearly the same sentiment as White's, and I appreciate the idea of reciprocity in friendship that my daughter has internalized. Friendship is more than a tremendous thing: In my daughter's mind, it is a gift given in actionable ways from one to another.

When asked, my daughter explained why she memorized the quote. She said simply it is because Charlotte the barn spider was good to her pig friend, Wilbur. Those who remember the novel might recall that Charlotte sacrifices much for the pig, devoting her short life to saving his. White's classic is about self-sacrificial love, the kind rare, good friends offer and perform—in works—for each other. It is the kind of love Jesus gives to us.

When my family experienced collective wonder at the Grand Canyon, the "Canyon" we ended up taking away together as Sandburg terms it, was not only awe at God's handiwork in nature but also his handiwork that we witnessed at work inside our daughter—handiwork forming her soul through children's literature that breathed beauty and truth into her heart without her parents or any other authority dictating it. We were affirmed that the words and stories we had read in communion with her had formed her soul. That is what happens when good literature is allowed to work in tandem with spiritual teaching and a religious life lived out. Importantly, the message about friendship is one my daughter needed to hear this year especially. It was tailored for her heart, and she heard it and shared it with all of us in a moment when we were all experiencing awe together. Shared reading brought our whole family closer not only to her and each other but also to God.

At the center of my family's Catholic lived experiences is, of course, Mass and the worship of our Lord. Adoration, praying the rosary, religious education, and other faith formation classes are also a regular part of our family's Catholic routines. By adding reading practices as part of our spiritual formation, we make room for the unexpected, the questions, the big feelings, the whys of God and our religion that come up not only when

---

2. White, *Charlotte's Web*, 139.

Epilogue

we expect and plan for them, but also when we don't. Reading as spiritual practice is a journey, an imperfect one, to be sure. Yet it is a wondrous, faith-filled adventure, one I hope this book has made exciting for you as you consider joining the adventure with my family.

This book has covered four themes: living liturgically, the interplay of faith and reason, cultivating a culture of life, and care of God's creation. There are many more to be explored in our Catholic faith, and I hope you are emboldened to find children's literature that you love that speaks to your children's hearts and what they, and perhaps you, most need to contemplate.

As St. Josemaria Escrivá reminds us, "Reading has made many saints."[3] And that is, after all, the goal of all our Catholic lives.

I invite you to enjoy and encounter reading children's books with the young people you love with a fresh perspective—and perhaps on your own too—as you explore how reading literature can open new avenues to discuss, understand, and deepen our communal relationship with our Catholic faith.

Enjoy reading wondrously!

---

3. Escrivá, "To Seek Christ."

Appendix

THIS COMPREHENSIVE APPENDIX IS crafted to serve as a helpful guide, offering a curated selection of books and discussion questions chosen to complement the themes of faith and Catholicism covered throughout *Wondrous Reading*. For each thematic chapter within this book, you'll find a list of additional texts that would work well to prompt conversations about that chapter's theme. Tailored for parents, caretakers, parish leaders, educators, librarians, and children's book lovers of all types, the carefully selected book lists aim to foster a shared love for literature and to build community—all while sparking discussions about the teachings of the Catholic faith.

Recognizing the diversity in age, maturity, and interests among readers, the lists below encourage flexibility. Customize your readings and how you choose to use them to align with the individual preferences, personalities, and maturity levels of your specific reading group. This will ensure a more impactful reading experience for all. In *The Read-Aloud Family*, Sarah Mackenzie reminds families that they ought to embrace the unexpected richness of reading picture books aloud with teens as she does, for instance.

As a college professor, I have likewise found that this age group enjoys—and responds thoughtfully to—picture books, in addition to longer chapter books. Thus, while age ranges are listed for each book title and sectional groupings below, don't feel bound by the age ranges publishers or educators have assigned to the texts. Rather, use them as guides and discover what works for you and your readers. Picture books might work well for teens, and chapter books in the middle-grade section below might work well for younger or older readers.

I invite you to let this appendix be a compass rather than a fixed path, providing additional options for you to consider as best fits for your purposes in catechizing youth through literature. This collection of books extends beyond those covered within the thematic book chapters, offering a wealth of selections suitable for faith discussions with children across elementary, middle-grade, and high school levels. You'll find concise book summaries, each accompanied by a discussion-initiating question and concluding with a set of overarching questions for general application. This appendix is a valuable tool for nurturing meaningful conversations rooted in the tenets of the Catholic faith. It aims to do more than assist you and the children you care about in accomplishing your collective reading goals; it invites you both to take part in vibrant conversations, hopefully making each turn of the page an exploration of the richness available between literature and spirituality.

Chapter 1: Liturgical Living in *Cecilia's Magical Mission* and *The Giving Tree*

This chapter introduces liturgical living to elementary-aged students through Shel Silverstein's enduring classic *The Giving Tree* (four–eight). For middle-grade readers, it delves into Viola Canales's *Cecilia's Magical Mission* (ten–fifteen), a novel that stresses the importance of the sacraments through a new and engrossing perspective.

Beyond the two books covered within the chapter, here are additional books and sample questions that might help readers to contemplate liturgical living in literature.

Elementary Selections (four–twelve years):

1. **The Tale of Three Trees** by Angela Elwell Hunt, illustrated by Tim Jonke (six–ten): A traditional folktale that has been adapted into various forms over the years. The beautifully illustrated picture-book version about three trees' aspirations offers lessons about God's plan and purpose for our lives.

    Question: Can you find how each tree's journey is like a special time in the church year, such as Advent, Christmas, or Easter?

2. **Nothing to Do** by Eric Russell Hoban, illustrated by Lillian Hoban (four–eight): In this classic and imaginative picture book, a young

Appendix

opossum's father gives him a "magic stone" to help his young child figure out what to do when he is bored.

> *Question:* In the story, the young opossum finds fun things to do with the magic stone when he's bored. How can we find fun and meaningful things to do during Ordinary Time, the part of the church year when we focus on growing in our everyday lives?

3. ***The Legend of St. Nicholas*** by Demi (four–ten): This beautifully illustrated picture book tells the story of St. Nicholas of Myra, beginning from when he was a child born around 280 AD in Turkey and detailing his spiritual destiny to become the patron saint of children.

   > *Question:* During Advent and Christmastide, we celebrate St. Nicholas. Why do you think children have a special role in liturgical living? How do you like to celebrate St. Nicholas with your family?

4. ***The Velveteen Rabbit*** by Margery Williams (four–twelve): A story about a toy rabbit's journey to become real through the power of love and the special magic that happens from being cherished by a child.

   > *Question:* How do you think the rabbit becoming "real" is like growing closer to God? You might recall that the rabbit was a gift during Christmastide.

5. ***Charlotte's Web*** by E. B. White (six–twelve): A timeless tale of friendship between a pig named Wilbur and a clever spider named Charlotte.

   > *Question:* Can you recall a time when you showed friendship or kindness to someone, like the creatures in the story? How do you think being a good friend is what Jesus tells us to do? How are you a good friend as a child in your "season of life"?

6. ***The Cricket in Times Square*** by George Selden (eight–twelve): An endearing tale set in the lively city of New York, where a musical cricket named Chester forms a friendship with a mouse and a cat. Through their adventures, they uncover the magic of camaraderie, perseverance, and the enchanting power of music in the heart of Times Square.

Question: How does the musical talent of Chester the cricket remind you of the music we hear in church during liturgical celebrations like Easter and Christmas? How does music affect the story's characters? How do you feel when you hear particular music?

7. ***The Little Flower: A Parable of St. Thérèse of Lisieux*** by Becky Arganbright (three–seven): This book introduces children to the life of St. Thérèse of Lisieux, a famous child saint.

    Question: How does the story of St. Thérèse of Lisieux and her "Little Way" inspire us to be good? How can we act like her? How do you think she celebrated the liturgical year?

Middle-Grade Selections (Ten–Fourteen):

1. ***Strawberry Girl*** by Lois Lenski (ten–fourteen): The story of Birdie Boyer, a girl in rural Florida, and her family's struggles and triumphs as they farm strawberries and work together to build a community with their neighbors.

    Question: In *Strawberry Girl*, Birdie and her family work hard and face challenges while growing strawberries. How can their perseverance remind us of the lessons we learn during the liturgical season of Lent, when we focus on self-discipline and spiritual growth? When do we see Birdie practicing self-discipline specifically, or doing what you know is right, even when you don't feel like doing it? When have you practiced self-discipline recently?

2. ***The Bronze Bow*** by Elizabeth George Speare (ten–fourteen): A compelling historical novel set in Roman-occupied Israel, following the story of a young man named Daniel who seeks to avenge his father's death but meets Jesus of Nazareth, a traveling carpenter, and learns an important lesson about forgiveness.

    Question: This book has us meet Jesus as a historical figure. How do you think you would react if you were in Daniel's shoes? Do you think this book should be read during Lent or Eastertide? Why? What lessons might it teach?

Appendix

3. ***The Door in the Wall*** by Marguerite de Angeli (eight–twelve): Set in medieval England, the novel follows a young boy named Robin who is expected to become a knight but suffers a tragedy. A monk rescues and mentors him, and Robin learns that being noble is about more than having physical strength.

    Question: The novel focuses on the cardinal virtue of fortitude. Where do you see this in the story? How does Robin's journey inspire you to face challenges? How is liturgical living aligned with the virtue of fortitude and the Catholic calendar?

4. ***The Family Under the Bridge*** by Natalie Savage Carson, illustrated by Garth Williams (six–twelve): Armand, an old man living on the streets of Paris, enjoys his solitary life until he discovers three cold and hungry children near his favorite spot just before Christmas. Despite his initial reluctance, Armand grows to care for the children and resolves to find them a real home.

    Question: During Advent, Mary and Joseph were without a place to sleep the night Jesus was born. How does the story about Armand and the children help you to appreciate what Mary and Joseph went through? How can you help others less fortunate during Advent and Christmastide?

5. ***The Great Brain*** by John D. Fitzgerald, originally illustrated by Mercer Mayer (seven–eleven): Set in the small town of Adenville, Utah, at the end of the nineteenth century, this autobiographical novel tells the story of Tom Dennis Fitzgerald, "The Great Brain," as recounted by his younger brother. The Fitzgerald family is Catholic, growing up in a predominantly Mormon town.

    Question: How do the Fitzgeralds live out their faith even in a community when they are not the main religion? Have you ever felt it was hard to live liturgically, for any reason?

6. ***Little House in the Big Woods*** by Laura Ingalls Wilder (eight–twelve): This series details the pioneer life of Laura Ingalls and her family as they navigate the American Midwest in the late 1890s.

Question: How do the different family members incorporate religious teachings and practices into their daily routines? Discuss a character's routine you liked best.

7. *The Green Ember* by S. D. Smith, illustrated by Zach Franzen (six–twelve): Heather and Picket, ordinary rabbits, are thrust into a world of chaos and adventure when unexpected events force them into a struggle involving kings, kingdoms, and tyrants.

   Question: During Lent, we are called as Catholics to deepen our faith through prayer, fasting, and almsgiving. How do you see Heather and Picket growing stronger in character throughout this book? How might we relate this to our Lenten journeys?

High School Selections (Fourteen–Eighteen):

1. *A Tree Grows in Brooklyn* by Betty Smith (fourteen–eighteen): This coming-of-age classic highlights sensitive Francie Nolan as she learns about life's joys and sorrows in the slums of New York at the turn of the twentieth century.

   Question: In *A Tree Grows in Brooklyn*, Francie and her family face hardships, but they also find moments of hope and joy. How can Francie's resilience and her family's ability to find joy in small things inspire us during the liturgical season of Advent, a time of hope and preparation?

2. *Kristin Lavransdatter* by Sigrid Undset (fourteen–eighteen): A historical novel trilogy that recounts the thrilling life of a woman living in fourteenth-century Norway. The narrative explores Kristin's coming of age, her relationships, and the challenges she faces against the backdrop of real historical events, including the Black Death.

   Question: Discuss or even write down some of the novel's portrayals of historical events and religious practices. How does it depict liturgical life? How do we as Catholics practice living liturgically in those same ways or differently now?

Appendix

3. ***The Song of Bernadette*** by Franz Werfel (fourteen–eighteen): This book dives into the story of St. Bernadette Soubirous and the Marian apparitions at Lourdes, exploring the themes of faith, miracles, and devotion.

   Question: What does Bernadette's experience with the Virgin Mary at Lourdes teach us about Catholic Marian devotion and liturgical spirituality? For reference, liturgical spirituality refers to a way of experiencing and expressing one's faith through liturgical living practices—or, practicing your faith by reverently observing the Catholic calendar and timekeeping.

4. ***The Power and the Glory*** by Graham Greene (fourteen–eighteen): A gripping novel that explores the complexities of faith, morality, and redemption through the journey of an alcoholic and disillusioned priest on the run in 1930s Mexico during a time of anti-Catholic persecution.

   Question: Note when doxology (a liturgical praise to God like Catholic prayers) is used in this book. Why do you think the novel uses doxology in the moments it does?

5. ***A Christmas Carol*** by Charles Dickens (fourteen–eighteen): In this timeless Advent and Christmastide classic, the miserly Ebenezer Scrooge is transformed after being visited by the ghosts of Christmas Past, Present, and Yet to Come.

   Question: Scrooge's biggest transformation is in his charity, or love. Charity is the greatest of all theological virtues. Find a specific moment when you see a change in Scrooge's attitude toward charity. You might refer to *The Catechism* sections 1822–1829 about charity for reference here.

6. ***The Story of a Soul*** by St. Thérèse of Lisieux (fourteen–eighteen): Discover the spiritual journey of St. Thérèse of Lisieux through her autobiographical writings. Read about the "Little Way" in her own words.

   Question: Can you identify specific instances in the book where St. Thérèse lives out the "Little Way"? How might these instances inspire a connection with liturgical living for her? How might the "Little Way" inspire you to live liturgically in a small, or little, way? What small change could you make in your life to live more liturgically?

7. **Cry, the Beloved Country** by Alan Paton (fourteen–eighteen): This novel explores the complexities of apartheid-era South Africa, delving into the story of two protagonists, a Black priest and a white farmer, as they journey to Johannesburg to connect with their sons.

   Question: Forgiveness is a prominent theme in the novel. How do the characters show forgiveness? How might their actions align with Catholic teachings on forgiveness and the pursuit of social justice? You might consider the redemptive power of the sacraments as you answer.

Liturgical Living: Broad Questions You Might Ask for Books for Children or Young Adults

1. How does the story connect with specific liturgical seasons, such as Advent, Christmastide, Lent, or Eastertide, or Ordinary Time? What aspects of the church calendar can be identified in the narrative? If obvious Catholic connections aren't there, how does the book's rhythm, pace, and specific traditions provide insight into the value of liturgical living?

2. How does the story depict the concept of community? In what ways does it reflect the communal aspects of liturgical living, such as shared celebrations, rituals, or acts of service?

3. Are there elements in the book that reflect sacramental themes, like the Eucharist, Baptism, or Confirmation? If so, how do they contribute to an understanding of the value of liturgical living?

4. Which virtues and vices are demonstrated by the characters? How might these align with the virtues emphasized in Catholic teachings? How do the book's characters help us to contemplate how best to lead a faith-filled life?

5. Are there moments in the story that delve into the challenges of faith or periods of spiritual growth? How might these reflect the ups and downs of the liturgical journey?

Appendix

Chapter 2: Faith and Reason in *Goodnight Moon* and the Magic Tree House Series

This chapter explored how faith and reason complement—and challenge—each other in stories for children and young adults, raising questions children often have about the role of faith in scholastic society, a space often considered secular. We look at the classic picture-book *Goodnight Moon* by Margaret Wise Brown (zero–six). The chapter also examines Mary Pope Osborne's Magic Tree House series (seven–twelve), where two siblings, Jack and Annie, learn about faith and the often-insatiable quest for knowledge. Using these texts, the chapter shows that even simple bedtime tales can touch on big ideas, especially when the power of illustrations—and iconography—are considered.

Beyond the two books covered within the chapter, here are some more books and sample questions that might help readers to contemplate faith and reason in literature.

Elementary Selections (Four–Twelve):

1. ***The Berenstain Bears and the Big Question*** by Jan Berenstain (four–eight): In this classic Berenstain Bears story, the cubs grapple with questions about faith and reason.

    Question: How do the Berenstain Bears characters handle their questions about faith and reason? Can you find examples of Catholic teachings in the story?

2. ***Stellaluna*** by Janell Cannon (four–nine): A heartwarming tale of a bat raised by birds, this book explores themes of acceptance and understanding in the face of differences.

    Question: What does Stellaluna learn about herself through her five senses, what she can see, taste, smell, hear, and touch? What about through faith, or what she senses to be true?

3. ***The Story of Ferdinand*** by Munro Leaf (four–eight): Follows the story of a gentle bull who prefers flowers to fighting.

Question: How does Ferdinand combine faith and reason to come to peace with his love for flowers? Is there anything you love like Ferdinand? Why do you think you love what you love?

4. ***Horton Hears a Who!*** by Dr. Seuss (four–eleven): A whimsical tale that follows Horton the elephant as he goes to great lengths to protect the tiny inhabitants of Whoville.

    Question: In Dr. Seuss's story, why is it important for Horton to protect the tiny Whos? How might this connect to what we hear in church about having faith in things we can't always see?

5. ***Where the Wild Things Are*** by Maurice Sendak (four–twelve): A beloved classic that explores the wild imagination of a young boy named Max, who is sent to his bedroom after getting in trouble. There, he sails to an island jungle where he meets mysterious Wild Things.

    Question: Why is it important to know the difference between what is true and not true in Max's story? How do you know?

6. ***The Tale of Peter Rabbit*** by Beatrix Potter (five–twelve): This story traces the mischievous Peter Rabbit as he learns valuable lessons about obedience and responsibility.

    Question: Peter Rabbit gets in a lot of trouble! How does he reason himself out of it? When is his reasoning wrong? When is it right?

7. ***The Best-Loved Doll*** by Rebecca Caudill, Illustrated by Elliot Gilbert (two–nine): A little girl named Betsy gets an invitation to bring her favorite doll Jennifer to a party to win a prize, and she learns that love is the best prize there is.

    Question: Betsy finds out her doll isn't perfect. What's reasonably "wrong" with Jennifer? Is anything wrong with her? Why does Betsy end up with faith that Jennifer's the best doll there is anyway? How is Besty's love for her doll like God's love for us?

Appendix

Middle-Grade Selections (Ten–Fourteen):

1. ***The Chronicles of Narnia: The Lion, the Witch, and the Wardrobe*** by C. S. Lewis (ten–fourteen): The well-known tale of four siblings who, through a magical wardrobe, find themselves in the wondrous land of Narnia, where they join forces with the noble lion Aslan to confront the White Witch and restore peace to the realm.

    Question: How might the wardrobe symbolize the marker between two lands, faith and reason? (You might even draw this one out!)

2. ***Holes*** by Louis Sachar (ten–fourteen): An unexpected and wry novel that focuses on Stanley Yelnats, a boy sent to a juvenile detention camp where he is forced to dig holes. While there, he learns secrets about the camp's past—and his family's.

    Question: We often reason out our bad choices. What do the boys learn from digging holes? What might the boys learn about sin in this novel? How might Camp Green Lake be like Purgatory?

3. ***Tuck Everlasting*** by Natalie Babbitt (ten–fourteen): A thought-provoking novel about a girl named Winnie Foster who discovers spring water that can offer immortality.

    Question: In *Tuck Everlasting*, Winnie encounters the idea of eternal life on Earth. Why do you think she chooses what she does at the end? How can our faith in Jesus as Catholics help guide us through the same struggles Winnie has? What is the faith and reason struggle in this book?

4. ***A Wrinkle in Time*** by Madeleine L'Engle (Ten–Fourteen): A science-fiction fantasy novel that follows the extraordinary journey of Meg Murry, her brother Charles Wallace, and their friend Calvin O'Keefe as they traverse space and time to rescue Meg's father from the clutches of an evil force using the mysterious concept of tesseracts.

    Question: How does the concept of time travel in *A Wrinkle in Time* parallel Catholic beliefs about the eternal nature of God and the spiritual realm beyond time?

5. ***Bridge to Terabithia*** by Katherine Paterson (ten–fourteen): A poignant tale of friendship, imagination, and coping with loss as friends Jess and Leslie create a magical kingdom in the woods.

   Question: In what ways does the friendship between Jess and Leslie reflect the Catholic values of compassion and understanding and the role of faith in overcoming challenges? What struggles with faith do the main characters have, and how might you overcome those as a Catholic reader?

6. ***Matilda*** by Roald Dahl (eight–twelve): Matilda, a gifted, young girl with telekinetic abilities, navigates a difficult home and school life.

   Question: Matilda's telekinetic abilities set her apart in the story. How might these extraordinary gifts be seen as a metaphor for the unique talents each person has? How does this reflect the concept of spiritual gifts in our Christian faith? How might the story teach us about using our gifts of reason and faith for good and evil?

7. ***Island of the Blue Dolphins*** by Scott O'Dell (ten–fourteen): Based on the true story of a Nicoleño Indian girl, this novel tells the tale of Karana, who survives alone for eighteen years on San Nicolas Island in the 1800s.

   Question: In what ways might Karana's journey in *Island of the Blue Dolphins* resonate with Catholic teachings on the resilience of the human spirit and navigating the balance between faith and reason in times of adversity? You might look up and reference the apostle Paul in Philippians 4:13 here.

High School Selections (Fourteen–Eighteen):

1. ***Fahrenheit 451*** by Ray Bradbury (fourteen–eighteen): This is a dystopian novel that explores a future society where books are banned and firemen burn any that are found. Protagonist Guy Montag grapples with the consequences of censorship and the suppression of intellectual freedom.

Appendix

Question: How does the dystopian society in *Fahrenheit 451* highlight the dangers of suppressing knowledge, and in what ways can this be connected to Catholic teachings on the importance of intellectual inquiry and the pursuit of truth? You might reference *The Catechism*, 27–30, 33 and 1776–1794 here.

2. ***The Giver*** by Lois Lowry (fourteen–eighteen): A thought-provoking novel that traces the story of Jonas, a young boy in a seemingly utopian society, who discovers the cost of conformity and the suppression of emotions.

    Question: How might *The Giver* help you to reflect on pursuing truth even when society tries to suppress it? What does Catholicism say about pursuing truth? What would you do in Jonas's situation? Have you ever experienced a moral situation like Jonas's on a smaller scale?

3. ***Brave New World*** by Aldous Huxley (fourteen–eighteen): This novel depicts a dystopian world where pleasure and stability take precedence over individuality and critical thinking, again prompting questions about faith and reason.

    Question: In what ways does *Brave New World* explore the dangers of choosing pleasure over critical thinking? How can this be connected to Catholic teachings on the balance between faith and reason? CCC 31–38 and 159 might be useful here.

4. ***The Fault in Our Stars*** by John Green (fourteen–eighteen): A heart-wrenching story of love between two teenagers, Hazel Grace Lancaster and Augustus Waters. They meet at a cancer support group and find themselves navigating illness, love, and the pursuit of meaning in a seemingly unjust world.

    Question: The novel delves into philosophical questions about the meaning of life and the impact of illness on one's sense of purpose. How do Hazel and Augustus deal with these questions? How do faith and reason come into play as the two characters contemplate the meaning of their lives and fleeting love? What would a specifically Catholic love story look like exploring these ideas? Would it be the same or different?

Wondrous Reading

5. ***The Book Thief*** by Markus Zusak (fourteen–eighteen): A tale set in Nazi Germany, narrated by Death. It follows Liesel Meminger as she steals books, finds solace in words during a time of war, and forms unexpected connections with her foster family and a Jewish fist-fighter hidden in their basement.

   Question: In what ways does Liesel Meminger's relationship with books and words reflect the power of literature to provide connection in the face of adversity? Have you ever considered a character in a book to be a friend? How does reading bring us together and help us to find truth? How might this book help us to think through what Catholicism says about suffering and truth? You might reference CCC 517, 606–18.

6. ***To Kill a Mockingbird*** by Harper Lee (fourteen–eighteen): In this powerful novel exploring racial injustice and moral growth in the American South during the 1930s, Scout Finch watches her father, Atticus, defend an innocent Black man accused of a crime.

   Question: What is Catholic social justice? You might look at CCC 1877–1889. How does this novel show ideas about Catholic social justice, and how does it not? How does Scout use her faith and reason to guide her in ideas about social justice? Does she rely on one more than the other? Do you?

7. ***The Lord of the Flies*** by William Golding (fourteen–eighteen): This coming-of-age story presents a harrowing tale about a group of boys who descend into savagery and chaos when stranded on a deserted island.

   Question: What decisions would you make were you to land on this island? Would they be the same as these boys? When and how would you have made different decisions exactly? Where do you see faith and/or reason gone awry, that is being skewed too far one way or another? Imagine what would happen on the island if the boys tried to make Catholic choices. Is there a boy already in the book you see doing that in some way? How so?

Appendix

Faith and Reason: Broad Questions You Might Ask for Any Books for Children or Young Adults

1. How does the story's portrayal of faith depict Catholic teachings about trusting God? In what ways does reason play a role in the characters' development?

2. Are there moral dilemmas that ask characters to rely on both faith and reason? How might these situations help us to think through Catholic teachings on moral discernment and the application of reason? As a reference point, Catholic moral discernment is the process of prayerful reflection and thoughtful consideration guided to make sound decisions aligned with the Church's principles. CCC 1176–1802 is a good reference for these types of questions.

3. Do the characters in the book encounter challenges or doubts that require faith and reason for resolution? How might these experiences parallel the struggles and questions often faced by people like us in our Catholic faith journeys?

4. Are there moments when characters engage in dialogue or discussion, hoping to reconcile differences of faith and reason? How can this reflect the Catholic commitment to respectful dialogue and intellectual engagement geared toward truth? Have you ever had a disagreement about faith and reason that has gone exceptionally well, or badly, like it does for the characters? What did you learn from what happened to you? What could you learn from what happens to the characters?

5. Are there elements in the book that explore the role of science or the natural world in shaping the characters' understanding of faith? How might these themes or moments help us to think through Catholic beliefs in exploring the natural order of the world through reason?

Chapter 3: The Culture of Life in *Alma and How She Got Her Name* and *Little Women*

The culture of life is explored in this chapter first in Juana Martinez-Neal's *Alma and How She Got Her Name* (three–nine). The heroine's journey of self-discovery and the symbolism of her long name combine in this picture book to emphasize the importance of relationships, both with the living and the dead. Cultivating a culture of life is also examined in Louisa May Alcott's beloved classic *Little Women* (eight–eighteen), which delves into the March sisters' loving and memorable lives.

Beyond the two books covered within the chapter, here are some more books and sample questions that might help readers to contemplate the culture of life in literature.

Elementary Selections (Four–Twelve):

1. ***The Rainbow Fish*** by Marcus Pfister (four–eight): This heartwarming tale follows the journey of a beautiful yet vain fish who learns that outward beauty does not win lasting friendships, but inner beauty can.

    Question: What does the Rainbow Fish's story teach us about how to build a loving community?

2. ***The Lion and the Mouse*** by Jerry Pinkney (four–nine): This wordless, yet beautifully illustrated picture book depicts an unlikely pair of animals, a lion and mouse, who look after each other even though they are usually at odds in the animal kingdom.

    Question: How does the relationship between the lion and the mouse show us to care about those different from us? Have you ever reached out to be a friend to someone different from you? Has anyone different from you ever reached out to be a friend to you?

3. ***The Empty Pot*** by Demi (four–eight): A Chinese tale about a boy named Ping who loves flowers but struggles to make a particular flower seed given to him by the emperor bloom.

    Question: Enjoying a culture of life in Catholicism is not just about humans. It's also about plants! How does the boy Ping show love to his plant? When have you shown a plant love?

4. ***Last Stop on Market Street*** by Matt de la Peña (four–nine): This book focuses on a young boy named CJ and his grandmother as they ride a bus across the city. Through different people and varied experiences, the story shines light on the beauty of diversity and how it is possible to find joy in unexpected places.

Appendix

Question: What kinds of different people do CJ and his grandmother meet on the bus around the city? How many different types of unique and wonderful people do you meet daily?

5. ***Each Kindness*** by Jacqueline Woodson, illustrated by E. B. Lewis (five–nine): This picture book shows what happens when a girl named Chloe and her friends refuse to play with Maya, a new girl at school. Their teacher intervenes to teach them about the ripple effect of kindness.

   Question: What kind acts do we see in the story that make a difference in the children's lives? What kind act could you do to make a difference in someone's life today?

6. ***Enemy Pie*** by Derek Munson (four–eight): This story follows a boy who learns a valuable lesson about friendship and understanding when his dad suggests making and sharing an "enemy pie" with a new friend.

   Question: How do the characters in the story show that they understand how others feel? What would you do if you had to share an "enemy pie" with someone?

7. ***Brother Hugo and the Bear*** by Katy Beebe, illustrated by S. D. Schindler (four–nine): Brother Hugo's library book, *The Letters of St. Augustine*, is devoured by a bear, leading him on a quest to replace it. He painstakingly recreates the manuscript from another copy. As he returns the borrowed book, the bear, who is now fond of letters, follows him. This leads to a funny and unexpected twist.

   Question: This book is based on a true story of a note found in a twelfth-century manuscript! How do you feel connected to the past as a reader and a Catholic after reading this story?

Middle-Grade Selections (Ten–Fourteen):

1. ***Esperanza Rising*** by Pam Muñoz Ryan (eight–fourteen): This compelling novel follows once wealthy and privileged Mexican immigrant Esperanza Ortega as she adapts to a new life of hardship and work in a farm camp in California during the Great Depression.

Question: How does the novel show Esperanza learning to help others before herself? You might consider her relationship to her family.

2. **The Mimosa Tree** by Vera and Bill Cleaver (eight–fourteen): Five children, abandoned by their stepmother after arriving in Chicago from North Carolina, attempt to support themselves and their blind father.

   Question: Marvella and her siblings make some bad choices when they feel as if they are abandoned. Have you ever felt this way? What could they have done differently? What should their stepmother have done differently? What about the government? What would a culture of life in this book look like from all involved?

3. **Out of My Mind** by Sharon M. Draper (ten–fourteen): This novel portrays the life of a girl with cerebral palsy, emphasizing the importance of understanding and inclusion, as well as recognizing the unique gifts of everyone.

   Question: How does the story teach us about the importance of understanding and including everyone, even if they're different from us? What did you learn about Sharon that surprised you? You might reference John 1–3 in thinking through these questions.

4. **The War That Saved My Life** by Kimberly Brubaker Bradley (nine–twelve): A historical novel that follows the story of Ada, a girl with a clubfoot, who, along with her brother Jamie, is evacuated from London to the English countryside during World War II.

   Question: What does this book teach about learning how to trust others? Have you been in a situation when you have found it hard to trust and make friendships or to be part of a community? What did you do?

5. **Wonder** by R. J. Palacio (eight–twelve): An incredible story about Auggie, a boy with facial differences who navigates the challenges of fitting in at a new school after being homeschooled for most of his childhood because of his differences.

Appendix

Question: Wonder is narrated by different characters. Who is your favorite and why? How does each character show the vibrancy of a culture of life?

6. ***The Borrowers*** by Mary Norton (eight–twelve): A family of tiny people, the Borrowers, live secretly in the walls and floors of an old house, surviving by borrowing items from humans.

   Question: How does the Borrowers' way of life reflect the Catholic value of respecting and protecting everyone, including the small and seemingly insignificant, in our world?

7. ***Pax*** by Sara Pennypacker (ten–fourteen): This novel explores the bond between a boy named Peter and his pet fox, Pax, who are separated due to war.

   Question: How does the story address the impact of war on people, both those in it and those affected by it? What lessons about valuing the sanctity, or sacredness, of life might we learn from this book? Do you know anyone who has ever been in a war? How did the experience affect them?

High School Selections (Fourteen–Eighteen):

1. ***The Hate U Give*** by Angie Thomas (fourteen–eighteen): A young adult novel that follows the life of Starr Carter, a Black teenager who witnesses the police shooting of her childhood friend, Khalil.

   Question: How is family and community highlighted as a value in this novel? Choose a specific moment when Starr is with a family member who is your favorite and talk about why this scene shows a culture of life.

2. ***All the Light We Cannot See*** by Anthony Doerr (fourteen–eighteen): A historical novel set during World War II. The story revolves around a blind French girl, Marie-Laure LeBlanc, and a German orphan, Werner Pfennig. As the war unfolds, their lives connect in unexpected ways.

Question: In what ways does the novel explore the idea of the unseen or hidden aspects of life, both in terms of the dangers during wartime and the potential for kindness and faith to emerge in unexpected places?

3. ***Between Shades of Gray*** by Ruta Sepetys (fourteen–eighteen): A historical fiction novel that recounts the story of a teenage girl named Lina, who, along with her family, is deported to Siberia by the Soviet Union during World War II.

   Question: How does the protagonist, Lina, use her artistic talents to cope with the hardships and injustices she faces during her deportation? How does this reflect the human capacity for resilience? How would you have acted in her circumstance?

4. ***Night*** by Elie Wiesel (fourteen–eighteen): A powerful memoir of Elie Wiesel's experiences in Nazi concentration camps, *Night* raises questions about the sanctity of life in the face of unimaginable atrocities.

   Question: How does *Night* invite you think differently about the sanctity of life because it is a memoir and not a fictional novel? How is it connected to the culture of life's commitment to human dignity? You might reference CCC 1700–1709 here.

5. ***Everything Sad is Untrue*** by Daniel Nayeri (fourteen–eighteen): A riveting, autobiographical novel about a young refugee's journey going from navigating politically tumultuous Iran to adjusting to home and school life in Oklahoma.

   Question: What does the book's title mean in relationship to the plot as a whole? How does its meaning reinforce the idea of a culture of life?

6. ***The Secret Life of Bees*** by Sue Monk Kidd (fourteen–eighteen): Set in 1960s South Carolina, the novel tells the story of Lily Owens and her journey to uncover the truth about the afternoon her mother was killed.

Appendix

Question: How does Lily's grief teach her to value her life and the lives of those closest to her more? Have you ever had an experience like hers with grief, or do you know someone who has?

7. **Anne of Green Gables** by L. M. Montgomery (fourteen–eighteen): A beloved classic about an imaginative orphan girl, Anne, who is adopted by a brother and sister on Prince Edward Island in Canada.

Question: How does Anne's imagination help her to appreciate life in ways others around her do not? How does she encourage others to appreciate life and see God's creation with wonder?

Culture of Life: Broad Questions You Might Ask for Any Books for Children or Young Adults

1. How does the book match up with Catholic teachings on the sacredness of human life from conception to natural death? How does it not?
2. Are there instances where characters demonstrate virtues emphasized in Catholic teachings, such as charity, compassion, or forgiveness? What about the opposite? Part 3 of *The Catechism*, "Life in Christ," is a good reference here, specifically the section "The Dignity of the Human Person," CCC 1803–1845.
3. Does the novel show the importance of the domestic church and convey family values in line with Catholic teachings? If not, how?
4. In what ways does the book incorporate Catholic values of justice and care for the marginalized? CCC 1807, 1928–1938, and 2443–2449 are helpful here.
5. Does the narrative include positive representations of family life and relationships? If not, what can we learn from the broken relationships in the book?

Chapter 4: Care of God's Creation in *The Snowy Day* and *The Wind in the Willows*

This chapter delved into the classic tales of Ezra Jack Keats's *The Snowy Day* (two–eight) and Kenneth Graham's *The Wind in the Willows* (eight–fourteen). These timeless works celebrate the beauty and wonder of the natural world, guiding readers toward an understanding of their role as stewards entrusted with caring for God's creation.

Beyond the two books covered within the chapter, here are some more books and sample questions that might help readers to contemplate care for God's creation in literature.

Elementary Selections (Four–Twelve):

1. ***Brother Sun, Sister Moon*** by Katherine Paterson (six–ten): This beautifully illustrated picture book captures the spirit of St. Francis of Assisi, highlighting the interconnectedness of all creation.

    Question: How does St. Francis's love for nature show us we should take care of God's creation? What's one thing you can do daily or weekly to show your love for the Earth (e.g., petting your dog, going on a walk, taking out the garbage)?

2. ***The Watcher*** by Nikki Grimes, illustrated by Bryan Collier (four–ten): Inspired by Psalm 21, this book shares the life of Jean-Michel Basquiat, an influential artist who found inspiration in the world around him.

    Question: How was Basquiat inspired to create art? What do you find beautiful in nature? What does nature's beauty inspire you to do creatively?

3. ***Miss Rumphius*** by Barbara Cooney (four–nine): A tale of a woman who aspired to make the world more beautiful by planting seeds everywhere she traveled.

    Question: How can you help make your neighborhood more beautiful like Miss Rumphius did?

4. ***The Salamander Room*** by Anne Mazer, illustrated by Steve Johnson and Lou Fancher (four–nine): A boy discovers a salamander in the woods and considers how he can make his room the perfect home for his new friend.

Appendix

Question: How does the boy show love for the salamander? Have you ever shown love for an animal in nature?

5. ***Boxcar Children: Tree House Mystery*** by Gertrude Chandler Warner (six–twelve): This short novel follows the adventures of four orphaned siblings—Henry, Jessie, Violet, and Benny Alden—who initially live in a boxcar, which they turn into their home, and who later are adopted by their grandfather. The Boxcar Children explore nature in this mystery installment while they also enjoy a tree house they build with their neighbors.

   Question: Why do you think the kids enjoy the tree house so much? How can your family and friends enjoy and learn from nature in your everyday lives? Do you have a secret hideout in nature, like a tree house? How is it different than a hideout or play area indoors?

6. ***The Little Engine That Could*** by Watty Piper (four–eight): This classic tale follows a small blue engine that takes on the challenging task of pulling a train over a mountain.

   Question: How does the Little Engine show us to use what we have wisely? How can you do the same to take care of God's creation?

7. ***The World Is Not a Rectangle: A Portrait of Architect Zaha Hadid*** by Jeanette Winter (six–ten): This picture book showcases Zaha Hadid's creative and beautiful architecture, inspiring discussions on sustainable and harmonious design.

   Question: How do Zaha Hadid's buildings show off God's creations? Are there any buildings in your neighborhood or community that you think show off God's creation?

Middle-Grade Selections (Ten–Fourteen):

1. ***Hatchet*** by Gary Paulsen (ten–fourteen): A thirteen-year-old boy, Brian Robeson, is the only survivor of a plane crash in the Canadian wilderness. Readers journey with him on his quest to stay alive.

Wondrous Reading

Question: Awe is respect mixed with wonder at God's creation. How does Brian's awe for nature grow while he is stranded? Point to a specific moment. Have you ever experienced any dangerous moments in nature when you felt awe?

2. ***My Side of the Mountain*** by Jean Craighead George (ten–fourteen): This is an adventurous tale about a resourceful young boy named Sam Gribley, who runs away from home to live in the Catskill Mountains of upstate New York. Sam relies on his survival skills and the companionship of a falcon named Frightful.

    Question: Throughout the story, how does Sam's relationship with the environment change? What lessons might you take away from his journey about the importance of respecting and preserving God's creation?

3. ***The Sign of the Beaver*** by Elizabeth George Speare (ten–fourteen): A historical novel that explores the friendship between two boys, a white settler named Matt and a Native American boy from the Beaver tribe named Attean, in eighteenth-century Maine.

    Question: Food and being hungry come up time and time again in this book. When he teaches Matt to fish, how is Attean also teaching about care of God's creation?

4. ***The One and Only Ivan*** by Katherine Applegate (eight–twelve): The story of a captive silverback gorilla named Ivan. Living in a mall, Ivan befriends other animals and, inspired by a baby elephant named Ruby, works toward a better life for himself and his friends.

    Question: How does Ivan's friendship with Ruby influence his perspective on captivity? How does he try to create a better life for the animals in the mall? Do you have animals you take care of? How do you try to make a better life for them?

5. ***Watership Down*** by Richard Adams (ten–fourteen): An epic adventure novel about a group of rabbits searching for a new home after their warren is destroyed.

Appendix

Question: In what ways does the natural world in *Watership Down* help the rabbits to survive and to shape their lives? How does the natural world shape your everyday life?

6. ***The Green Book*** by Jill Paton Walsh (ten–fourteen): Pattie and her family flee a dying Earth on a spaceship, but the new planet they land on, Shine, does not seem to have food to sustain them. The novel traces their survival adventure.

    Question: How does the novel explore taking our natural resources for granted? Are there any resources you take for granted that you might now think to take better care of after reading this book?

7. ***The Secret Garden*** by Frances Hodgson Burnett (eight–twelve): This classic novel follows Mary Lennox as she discovers a neglected, hidden garden on her uncle's estate.

    Question: Mary goes from being selfish to being charitable or loving. How does tending to the garden help her to change? Has being outside ever helped to make you more loving?

High School Selections (Fourteen–Eighteen):

1. ***The Overstory*** by Richard Powers (fourteen–eighteen): Winner of the 2019 Pulitzer Prize, this novel weaves together the stories of individuals connected by their love for trees.

    Question: What connection with trees did you find most relatable here? Do you have a favorite tree? What story would you tell about it?

2. ***Of Mice and Men*** by John Steinbeck (fourteen–eighteen): This classic novella recounts the lives of George Milton and Lennie Small, two displaced migrant ranch workers seeking job opportunities in California during the Great Depression.

    Question: In *Of Mice and Men*, how do the characters' actions toward animals and the land reflect their understanding of and respect for God's creation? Try to focus on one or two examples to make your case.

3. ***The Call of the Wild*** by Jack London (fourteen–eighteen): This exciting adventure novel tells the story of Buck, a domesticated dog who is stolen from his comfortable home and thrust into the harsh realities of the Alaskan wilderness.

   Question: In *The Call of the Wild*, we see nature and instinct through a dog's eyes. How does this perspective shed light on God's natural order? Does it help you to think through your relationship with animals you've been around? How might it?

4. ***The Lorax*** by Dr. Seuss (six–eighteen): The story revolves around the Once-ler, who heedlessly exploits the Truffula trees, leading to environmental degradation. The Lorax, a creature who speaks for the trees, tries to protect the ecosystem.

   Question: Explore the Once-ler's actions in the story. What are the consequences of his unchecked greed? How does the book convey a cautionary tale about the impact of human activities on the environment?

5. ***The Martian*** by Andy Weir (fourteen–eighteen): This book is an exciting science fiction tale that traces the story of Mark Watney, an astronaut stranded on Mars after a mission goes awry.

   Question: How does the astronaut's survival on Mars require resourcefulness and environmental sustainability? How can we apply these concepts on Earth for our continued survival? What thoughts would have been in the front of your mind as a Catholic astronaut that aren't perhaps in the front of his?

6. ***Wuthering Heights*** by Emily Brontë (fourteen–eighteen): Set against the backdrop of the Yorkshire moors, this sweeping gothic novel explores the intense and destructive love between Heathcliff and Catherine.

   Question: The moors matter in this story as much as the characters themselves to the book's development. Why do you think

Appendix

Heathcliff and Catherine are affected by their environment emotionally? When have you been affected by your environment emotionally in some way?

7. ***Pilgrim at Tinker Creek*** by Annie Dillard (fourteen–eighteen): This book relays the author's reflections on nature, existence, and the interconnectedness of life during an exciting year living along Tinker Creek in Virginia's Blue Ridge Mountains.

    Question: How does Annie Dillard's reflective journey in *Pilgrim at Tinker Creek* inspire readers to see God's creation with fresh eyes? How can we look at our own neighborhoods with similar, wonder-filled eyes?

Care of God's Creation: Broad Questions You Might Ask for Any Books for Children or Young Adults

1. How does the story encourage us to show gratitude for the beauty within God's creation? How can we show appreciation for nature's gifts in our daily lives?

2. In what ways do the characters in the book demonstrate responsible stewardship of the environment? How can we, like they, care for God's creation in our homes and communities? If they do not exhibit responsible stewardship, what do we learn?

3. In Catholicism, awe is a deep and reverential recognition of the divine majesty. It inspires a sense of wonder, humility, and adoration before the mysteries of God. Where do you see awe in the book? What do the characters learn from the awe-filled experience you've found? When have you experienced awe, and what did you learn?

4. Pope Francis often criticizes "throwaway culture," which he defines as a society that discards people and goods without considering their intrinsic value or the environmental impact. What specific actions or choices do the book's characters make to protect and nurture the environment? How can we incorporate similar actions and resist "throwaway culture"?

5. Does the book incorporate any elements of prayer, reflection, or spiritual connection with God's creation? When and where? How can we

integrate prayer into our own experiences with nature, fostering a deeper appreciation for God's gifts?

In the 1993 movie *Shadowlands*, William Nicholson as C. S. Lewis states, "We read to know we are not alone." *Wondrous Reading* invites book lovers of all ilks to explore imaginative reading alongside the riches of the Catholic faith. I hope you discover new books within this appendix and reconsider old ones with a fresh lens. As you read these books in communion with those you care about, I hope you spark a shared love for literature that broadens and deepens your faith experience in ways you had not heretofore considered. May *Wondrous Reading* be your key to traveling the world, to unlocking captivating stories that illuminate the path of faith not only for child and young adult readers but also for those readers like you who read with them as guides—those readers like you who know already the power that books can hold over our emotional, intellectual, and spiritual lives.

Bibliography

Alcott, Louisa May. *Little Women*. Children's Classics. Illustrations by Frank T. Merrill. New York: Random House, 1987.
Ansorge, Rick. "Piaget's Stages of Development." WebMD. https://www.webmd.com/children/piaget-stages-of-development.
Augustine. *The Confessions*. 2nd ed. Translated by F. J. Sheed. Introduction by Peter Brown. Indianapolis: Hackett, 2002.
Bertanzetti, Eileen Dunn. *Listening to God with Padre Pio*. Huntington: Our Sunday Visitor, 2011.
Blair, Elizabeth. "*Goodnight Moon* has Comforted Kids at Bedtime for 75 Years." *Morning Edition*, NPR, September 3, 2018. https://www.npr.org/2018/09/03/643249092/goodnight-moon-has-comforted-kids-at-bedtime-for-75-years.
Brody, Paul. *Biography of Kenneth Grahame*. N.p.: Golgotha, 2015. https://www.google.com/books/edition/The_Life_and_Works_of_Kenneth_Grahame/rv_wBgAAQBAJ?hl=en&gbpv=0.
Brown, Margaret Wise, and Clement Hurd. *Goodnight Moon*. New York: HarperOne, 2007.
Bulinski, Katherine. "Science, Truth, and Disaffiliation." *Church Life Journal*, December 7, 2023. https://churchlifejournal.nd.edu/articles/science-truth-and-disaffiliation/.
Canales, Viola. *Cecilia's Magical Mission*. Houston: Arte Público, 2022.
Carey, Joanna. "Inga Moore: Illustrating *The Wind in the Willows*." *The Guardian*, February 6, 2010. https://www.theguardian.com/books/2010/feb/06/inga-moore-illustration-wind-willows#:~:text=When%20The%20Wind%20in%20theRackham%20being%20the%20best%20known.
Catholic Church. *Catechism of the Catholic Church*. 2nd ed. Washington, DC: United States Conference of Catholic Bishops, 2011. http://www.usccb.org/beliefs-and-teachings/what-webelieve/catechism/catechism-of-the-catholic-church/epub/index.cfm.
———. *Nicene Creed*. Washington, DC: United States Conference of Catholic Bishops, n.d. https://www.usccb.org/beliefs-and-teachings/what-we-believe.
Centers for Disease Control and Prevention. "Mental Health Surveillance Among Children—United States, 2013–2019." *Morbidity and Mortality Weekly Report* 71, Suppl 2 (February 25, 2022) 1–42. https://www.cdc.gov/mmwr/volumes/71/su/su/7102a1.htm.

Bibliography

Children's Lifetime. "Data and Statistics on Children's Mental Health." https://www.childrenslifetime.org/long-term-effects.

Clark, Beverly Lyon. *The Afterlife of Little Women*. Baltimore: Johns Hopkins University Press, 2014.

Clark, Christina, Irene Picton, and Martin Galway. "Reading Trends 2023." National Literacy Trust, September 2023. https://cdn.literacytrust.org.uk/media/documents/Reading_trends_2023_G6DVx3V.pdf.

Crawford, Amy. "The Surprising Ingenuity Behind *Goodnight Moon*." *Smithsonian Magazine*, January 26, 2017. https://www.smithsonianmag.com/history/surprising-ingenuity-behind-goodnight-moon-180961923.

D'Amico, LuElla. "The Spiritual Life of Children During Pandemics." *Church Life Journal*, McGrath Institute for Church Life, University of Notre Dame, April 27, 2020. https://churchlifejournal.nd.edu/articles/the-spiritual-life-of-children-during-pandemics/.

Dovey, Ceridwen. "Can Reading Make You Happier?" *The New Yorker*, June 9, 2015. https://www.newyorker.com/culture/cultural-comment/can-reading-make-you-happier.

Escrivá, Josemaría. "To Seek Christ." July 11, 2002. https://escriva.org/en/camino/116/.

Fox, Mem. *Reading Magic: Why Reading Aloud to Our Children Will Change Their Lives Forever*. Illustrated by Judy Horacek. Updated and rev. ed. Boston: Harcourt, 2001.

Francis of Assisi. "The Canticle of Creation." *AllCreation.org*, May 5, 2024. https://www.allcreation.org/home/stfrancis-canticle.

Francis, Pope. "Catechesis on Prayer–28. Praying in Communion with the Saints." April 7, 2021. https://www.vatican.va/content/francesco/en/audiences/2021/documents/papa-francesco_20210407_udienza-generale.html

———. *Evangelii Gaudium*. Apostolic Exhortation, November 24, 2013. https://www.vatican.va/content/francesco/en/apost_exhortations/documents/papa-francesco_esortazione-ap_20131124_evangelii-gaudium.html.

———. *Laudato Si'*. Encyclical letter, May 24, 2015. https://www.vatican.va/content/francesco/en/encyclicals/documents/papa-francesco_20150524_enciclica-laudato-si.html.

Grahame, Kenneth. *The Wind in the Willows*. New York: Charles Scribner's Sons, 1908. https://www.sas.upenn.edu/~cavitch/pdf-library/Grahame_Wind_in_the_Willows_1908.pdf

Greeley, Andrew. *The Catholic Imagination*. Berkeley: University of California Press, 2000.

Hartwick, John, and Joyce Logan. "Teaching and Talking about Religion in Public Schools." In *Finding Common Ground: A First Amendment Guide to Religion and Public Schools*, edited by Charles C. Haynes, Oliver Thomas, et al., 171–78. Nashville: First Amendment Center, 2001.

John Paul II, Pope. *Evangelium Vitae [The Gospel of Life]*. Encyclical letter, March 25, 1995. https://www.vatican.va/content/john-paul-ii/en/encyclicals/documents/hf_jp-ii_enc_25031995_evangelium-vitae.html.

———. *Fides et Ratio*. Encyclical Letter on the Relationship between Faith and Reason. https://www.vatican.va/content/john-paul-ii/en/encyclicals/documents/hf_jp-ii_enc_14091998_fides-et-ratio.html.

Kalabekova, Inessa. "Viewing of the Painting as Deep Emotional Experience: A Martyr of Art, Mark Rothko." *Medium*. https://medium.com/@inessakalabekova/viewing-of-the-painting-as-deep-emotional-experience-a-martyr-of-art-mark-rothko-e3edf9fd5a2e.

Bibliography

Kamiya, Gary. "*The Wind in the Willows* Celebrates a Century." Salon.com, December 16, 2008. https://www.salon.com/2008/12/16/wind_in_the_willows/.

Keats, Ezra Jack. *The Snowy Day*. New York: Viking, 1962.

L'Engle, Madeleine. "Dare to Be Creative! A Lecture Presented at the Library of Congress." November 16, 1983. https://files.eric.ed.gov/fulltext/ED556901.pdf.

———. *Walking on Water*. New York: Crown, 2016.

Lewis, C. S. "On Three Ways of Writing for Children." In *"On Stories" and Other Essays on Literature*, 31–44. New York: HarperOne, 1982.

Mackenzie, Sarah. *The Read-Aloud Family: Making Meaningful and Lasting Connections with Your Kids*. Grand Rapids: Zondervan, 2018.

Magic Tree House Teachers Club. "Celebrating 25 Years." Magic Tree House Classroom Adventures. https://www.mthclassroomadventures.org/blog/celebrating-25-years.

Mar, Raymond A., Keith Oatley, Maja Djikic, and Justin Mullin. "Emotion and Narrative Fiction: Interactive Influences Before, During, and After Reading." *Cognition and Emotion* 25, no. 5 (2011) 818–33. https://doi.org/10.1080/02699931.2010.515151.

Maritain, Jacques. *Art and Scholasticism*. Translated by Joseph W. Evans, 1935. https://www3.nd.edu/~maritain/jmc/etext/art5.htm.

Martinez-Neal, Juana. *Alma and How She Got Her Name*. Somerville: Candlewick, 2018.

McCarty, Robert J., and John M. Vitek. *Going, Going, Gone: The Dynamics of Disaffiliation in Young Catholics*. Winona, MN: St. Mary's, 2018.

Michaels, Julia, and Benjamin Rice. "I'm a Star." From the movie *Wish*.

Muñoz Ryan, Pam. *Esperanza Rising*. New York: Scholastic, 2000.

Newton, John. "Amazing Grace." https://www.hymnal.net/en/hymn/h/313.

O'Malley, Timothy. *Becoming Eucharistic People: The Hope and Promise of Parish Life*. Notre Dame: Ave Maria, 2022.

Osborne, Mary Pope. *Dinosaurs Before Dark*. Illustrated ed. New York: Random House, 1992.

Paterson, Katherine. *Brother Son, Sister Moon*. Illustrated by Pamela Dalton. San Francisco: Chronicle, 2011.

Penguin Australia. "Classic of the Month: *Little Women*." https://www.penguin.com.au/articles/2899-classic-of-the-month-little-women.

Sandburg, Carl. "Many Hats." In *The Complete Poems of Carl Sandburg*, Introduction by Archibald MacLeish, 434. New York: Harcourt Brace Jovanovich, 1970.

Scholastic. "Scholastic Kids and Family Reading Report." https://www.scholastic.com/content/corp-home/kids-and-family-reading-report.html

Schultz, Colin. "The Pope Would Like You to Accept Evolution and the Big Bang." *The Smithsonian Magazine*, October 28, 2014. https://www.smithsonianmag.com/smart-news/pope-says-evolution-is-real-and-god-is-no-wizard-180952341/.

Silverstein, Shel. *The Giving Tree*. New York: Harper & Row, 1964.

Smith, Dinitia. "How 'Little Women' Got Big." *The New Yorker*, August 27, 2018. https://www.newyorker.com/magazine/2018/08/27/how-little-women-got-big.

Smith, James K. A. *Desiring the Kingdom: Worship, Worldview, and Cultural Formation*. Grand Rapids: Baker Academic, 2009.

Stewart, Haley. *The Grace of Enough: Pursuing Less and Living More in a Throwaway Culture*. Notre Dame: Ave Maria, 2018.

Teigen, Chrissy (@chrissyteigen). "[C]an't read the giving tree without crying, despite having read it 100 times. What is the moral here?" X, May 4, 2016. https://x.com/chrissyteigen/status/740730317305090048.

Bibliography

St. Thérèse of Lisieux. *My Catholic Life.* https://mycatholic.life/books/story-soul-saint-therese-lisieux/.

Trelease, Jim. *Read-Aloud Handbook.* 8th ed. Edited and revised by Cyndi Giorgis. New York: Penguin, 2019.

Vatican News. "Pope Francis: Rediscover the Value of Human Life." April 29, 2022. https://www.vaticannews.va/en/pope/news/2022-04/pope-francis-rediscover-the-value-of-family-life.html.

White, E. B. *Charlotte's Web.* New York: Harper & Brothers, 1952.

Wink, Joan. *The Power of Story.* Santa Barbara: ABC–Clio, 2017.

Index

Advent, 26, 37 39, 41, 114–15, 117–18, 120
Alcott, Abigail, 79
Alcott, Bronson, 79
Alcott, Louisa May, 73, 79, 81–85, 88, 141
Alma and How She Got Her Name, 23, 66, 72–73, 87–88, 97, 127, 143
"Amazing Grace," 143
Anne of Green Gables, 10, 133
Applegate, Katherine, 136
Aunt March, 82, 84–85
Ansorge, Rick, 141
anti-Catholic persecution, 119
Augustine, 62, 129, 141

Babbitt, Natalie, 123
Because of Winn Dixie, 93
beliefs, 30, 44, 46, 54, 69, 94, 123, 127
Best-Loved Doll, 122
The Best Worst Christmas Pageant Ever, 39
Bethlehem, 69
Black Death, 118
Borrowers, 131
Boxcar Children, 135
Boyer, Birdie, 116
Brave New World, 125
The Bridge to Terabithia, 8, 124
Bronze Bow, 116
Buliniski, Katherine, 47
Burnett, Frances Hodgson, 137

Caldecott Award, 72
The Call of the Wild, 137–38
Canales, Viola, 34, 114
Cannon, Janell, 121
Canticle of Creation, 91, 93, 105, 142
Carle, Eric, 92
Catechism of the Catholic Church, 14, 28, 37, 39, 141
The Catholic Imagination, 22, 142
Catholic Marian devotion, 119
Catholic Mass, 45
Catholic Social Teaching, 11
Caudill, Rebecca, 122
Cavaletti, Sofia, 92
Cecilia's Magical Mission, 23, 26, 34–41, 114
Charlotte's Web, 10, 93, 109–10, 115, 144
childlike belief, 44
Children's Classics, 141
Christmas Carol, 119
Christmas story, 69, 83
Christmastide, 37, 69, 81, 115, 117, 119–20
The Chronicles of Narnia, 10, 57, 123
Cleary, Beverly, 17
The Confessions, 62, 141
Cricket in Times Square, 115
culture, 47, 68, 80, 84, 86, 97, 132
Cry, the Beloved Country, 120

Dahl, Roald, 124
Dalton, Pamela, 91, 143

Index

DiCamillo, Kate, 93
Dickens, Charles, 119
Dillard, Annie, 139
Dinosaurs Before Dark, 57–61, 143
Disaffiliation, 47, 141
Disney, 59, 68–69, 78
Doerr, Anthony, 131
Door in the Wall, 117

Eastertide, 116, 120
Ebenezer Scrooge, 119
Epiphany, 37, 42
Esperanza Rising, 11–12
Eucharist, 120
Evangelii Gaudium, 80, 142
Evangelium Vitae, 67, 83, 86, 142

Family Under the Bridge, 117
Fahrenheit 451, 124–25
Fides et Ratio, 61, 142
Foster, Winnie, 123
Fox, Mem, 87
Francie Nolan, 118
Francis (Pope), 13–14, 20, 46, 80–81, 92–96, 98, 100, 102, 104–5, 139
Franzen, Zach, 118

Generation Z, 68
The Giver, 125
The Giving Tree, 23, 26–27, 30, 32–35, 38, 40, 114, 143
Golding, William, 126
Goodnight Moon, 23, 43, 49–52, 54–56, 58, 60, 62–64, 121, 141–42
Grahame, Kenneth, 101, 141
Greeley, Andrew, 22, 142
Greene, Graham, 119
Green Ember series, 118

"How Great Thou Art," 56
Hurd, Clement, 50, 56, 141
Huxley, Aldous, 125

Immaculate Heart, 75–77, 89
Island of the Blue Dolphins, 124

John Paul II (Pope), 67–68, 70, 80, 83, 86

Keats, Ezra Jack, 143
Kristin Lavransdatter, 118

Last Stop on Market Street, 128
L'Engle, Madeleine, 105, 123
Lenski, Lois, 116
Lent, 116, 118, 120
Lewis, C. S., 57–58, 123, 140, 143
Little Flower, 116
Little House in the Big Woods, 117
Little House on the Prairie series, 19
Little Women, 23, 66, 72–73, 79–90, 127–28, 141, 143
liturgical celebrations, 116
liturgical living, 5, 26–41, 72, 79, 114–15, 119–20, 128
The Lord of the Rings, 10
Lowry, Lois, 125
Luke's Gospel, 78

Mackenzie, Sarah, 4, 18, 113, 143
Magic Tree House Classroom Adventures, 143
Magic Tree House series, 20, 23, 43, 49, 57–58, 60–63
Magic Tree House Teachers Club, 57, 143
Marmee, 81–85
Martinez-Neal, Juana, 72–73, 78, 127, 143
Matilda, 124
Merrill, Frank T., 141
Milne, A.A., 96

Nayeri, Daniel, 132
Newbery Medal, 91
Nicene Creed, 55, 141
Noah, 41

O'Dell, Scott, 124
Of Mice and Men, 137
Ordinary Time, 26, 115, 120
Osborne, Mary Pope, 57, 143
Our Sunday Visitor, 141

Index

Palacio, R. J., 130
Paton, Alan, 120
Peter Pan, 10
Peter Rabbit, 122
Piaget, Jean, 15
Pigeon series, 93
Pilgrim at Tinker Creek, 139
Potter, Beatrix, 122
Power and the Glory, 119
Prince Warrior series, x

Rainbow Fish, 128
The Read-Aloud Family, 4–5, 18–19, 113, 143
Read-Aloud Handbook, 17–18, 144
Robinson, Barbara, 39
Rothko, Mark, 53, 143
Ryan, Pam Muñoz, 129

Sachar, Louis, 123
sanctification, 80
Sandburg, Carl, 109, 143
Scholastic, 17, 48, 143
Secret Garden, 20, 137
Selden, George, 115
Shadowlands, 140
Smith, Betty, 118
Smith, James K. A., 16, 143
Smith, S. D., 118
The Snowy Day, 23, 96–102, 105–6, 133, 143
social media influencers, 68
Song of Bernadette, 119
Speare, Elizabeth George, 116, 136

Stellaluna, 121
St. Nicholas, 115
St. Peter, 101
Strawberry Girl, 116
St. Thérèse of Lisieux, 78

Tale of Three Trees, 114
Taylor, Mildred D., 48
Treasure Island, 8
A Tree Grows in Brooklyn, 118
Trelease, Jim, 17–18
Tuck Everlasting, 123

Undset, Sigrid, 118

The Velveteen Rabbit, 8, 115
The Very Hungry Caterpillar, 92

Warner, Susan, 79
What Katy Did, 79
Where the Wild Things Are, 122
White, E.B., 109
White Witch, 123
The Wide, Wide World, 79
Wise Men, 69–70
Wilder, Laura Ingalls, 117
Willems, Mo, 93
The Wind in the Willows, 23, 91, 96–97, 101–7, 133, 141–43
Winnie the Pooh series, 96
Wise Brown, Margaret, 49–50, 121
Woolsey, Chauncey Sarah, 79
A Wrinkle in Time, 123
Wuthering Heights, 138